FRIENDLY FACES

[Frontispiece

THE SECOND BARON TAUCHNITZ

FRIENDLY FACES

OF THREE NATIONALITIES

BY

MISS M. B. BETHAM-EDWARDS

> " Fresh and strong the world we seize,
>   Pioneers, oh, pioneers ! "—WALT WHITMAN.

WITH PORTRAITS AND OTHER ILLUSTRATIONS

Essay Index Reprint Series

BOOKS FOR LIBRARIES PRESS
FREEPORT, NEW YORK

First Published 1911
Reprinted 1969

LIBRARY OF CONGRESS CATALOG CARD NUMBER:
69-17574

PRINTED IN THE UNITED STATES OF AMERICA

INSCRIBED TO

THE HONOURED MEMORY OF

THAT TRUE FRIEND OF LITERATURE AND

INTERNATIONAL FRIENDSHIP,

THE FIRST BARON TAUCHNITZ.

NOTE PREFATORY

Some of these sketches have appeared in English and American periodicals, others are now published for the first time. I make no apology for the introduction of one living personage into a little portrait gallery devoted to figures mostly long passed away. The founder of the Salvation Army may be said to have belonged to history for already a quarter of a century.

My best thanks are due to R. D. Cooper, Esq., of Needham Market, for kindly permitting a photograph of the cartoon in the apple-chamber, also to Mr. A. White, photographic artist, Ipswich, for his admirable reproduction of the same. The Suffolk views were taken for me by his late father a few years ago. The portrait of W. J. Fox was presented to me (1868–70) by his daughter, the late Mrs. G. Fox.

CONTENTS

LIST OF ILLUSTRATIONS

I

BARON TAUCHNITZ—A PRINCE OF PIONEERS

B

I

BARON TAUCHNITZ

PLEASANT as is the recollection of intercourse on paper with the House of Tauchnitz, that of a sojourn under its princely and hospitable roof must be counted among the red-letter days of literary life. Every circumstance connected with this great publishing firm brings agreeable associations to my mind. If a tribute to the living affords satisfaction, equally so does the opportunity of acquitting a debt of gratitude to the dead!

It was the late George Henry Lewes who introduced me, then a young writer, to the first Baron Tauchnitz. Ever kindness itself, readiest of the ready to encourage conscientious workers, he gave me a letter of introduction which I presented on my first visit to Leipzig in 1871. Since that time my works have regularly appeared from the Tauchnitz press, greatly to my own advantage, and, as I hope, not without amusement and instruction to continental readers. One fact let me affirm. Had Baron Tauchnitz never paid

English authors a penny, their gain would all the same have been immense. He obtained for them a vast, an unimaginably vast public. No author, says "the wise-browed Goethe," should write unless he can count his readers by the million. The Leipzig press brings us our million!

I was staying at Eisenbach in 1880 when an invitation reached me from Schloss Kleinschocher. Nothing could be more agreeable than the prospect of two or three days in a country house just then. The season was June, woods and breezy walks lie within reach of Luther's town, but the place itself was becoming hot, crowded, and noisy. Pianoforte practice rendered the hotel insupportable by day, and supper-parties in the gardens adjoining made sleep impossible till long past midnight. At the Leipzig station Baron Tauchnitz met me, little changed since I had seen him just ten years before. But for the slight accent of his otherwise excellent English, you might have taken the great publisher to be an English country gentleman. Half-an-hour's drive through a pleasant country brought us to a mansion worthy of a more musical name.

I was never in a more beautiful house; far and

[*To face p.* 4

THE FIRST BARON TAUCHNITZ

wide stretches a wooded park, whilst immediately around are flower-gardens and sweeps of turf so velvety as to recall our own lawns. And everything is of a piece within. We realise at once that we are not only in a most sumptuous home, but in one of the happiest and most cultured. Not that luxury is allowed to lend a material aspect. At Schloss Kleinschocher we breathe a literary atmosphere as completely as in the modest drawing-rooms of savants and littérateurs at Leipzig. On the tables of salon and boudoir lay the latest and best works in English, French, and German. The hostess, a grey-haired, tall, graceful lady with very gentle manners, and her daughter who welcomed me so kindly—alas! with her parents this dearly-loved daughter is no longer among the living—testified by their conversation to the widest culture. When Baron Tauchnitz—then the younger—with his charming wife joined us at the two-o'clock family dinner, we talked—and, of course, in English—of books, music, and the drama. The drama, indeed, forms so important an element in German life that it may be said to be part of daily existence. Baron Tauchnitz with a smile soon reminded me of this, and also of another fact, namely, of his excellent memory.

"When you stayed in Leipzig," he said (just ten years before), "you witnessed *Lohengrin*. To-night, if agreeable, my daughter will accompany you to see *Preciosa*."

True enough, a seat in the Tauchnitz opera-box had been placed at my disposal on my former visit, and in company of the Baron and his son I had then enjoyed a first-rate performance of Wagner's opera, but it surprised me to find the incident remembered by one so busy. A stroll in the gardens, a visit from the grandchildren, tea, and the opera, filled that first pleasant day at Schloss Kleinschocher—Schloss Tauchnitz, I feel inclined to call it.

"Now you shall see *my* library, the real Tauchnitz library," said my host next morning, leading me to a large, handsome room, devoted to the 3,040 volumes known under that name. At the time I write of the number was much less, but already made a goodly show, the little volumes being all neatly yet handsomely bound in maroon calf with gilt lettering and edges, and placed in a handsome bookcase reaching from floor to ceiling. Truly the Baron has reason to be proud of his library—now doubled; what author of voluminous works more so? No English-speaking person, least of all a contributor to the series, can gaze on this collection without feelings of pride and pleasure.

There are two circumstances especially to be borne in mind when reviewing Baron Tauchnitz's achievement: first and foremost, the originality of the undertaking; secondly, the high principles on which it has ever been conducted. When the felicitous notion of popularising English literature on the Continent first entered the Baron's mind, the only means of procuring an English book was to write to London for it. No international copyright existed, consequently any foreign publisher could reissue works printed in this country without asking an author's permission, to say nothing of paying for the privilege. Baron Tauchnitz entertained too much respect for literature in general, and for English literature in particular, to dream of such a system. He preferred the open, the magnanimous course, thereby not only furthering the progress of international intercourse, but paving the way for international copyright. The little Tauchnitz volume, so portable, so inexpensive, so well printed, forms a kind of literary currency: it prevents the English resident abroad from feeling exiled; it passes from hand to hand, spreading a knowledge alike of our classics and contemporary authors; lastly, it has been a powerful protest against the piratical principle, the notion that sharpness in business may well take the place of straightforward dealing. To authors the gain has been twofold, the Baron not only adding very considerably to their incomes, but also establishing their reputation on the Continent.

Hardly less interesting than his Tauchnitz library at Schloss Kleinschocher is my host's collection of portraits and autograph letters. The photos of many English authors are here, whilst from all whose works are included in the Continental Series the Baron has received letters.

Take the following Sternean line from Thackeray—

"Don't be afraid of your English; a letter containing £ s. d. is always in pretty style."

Equally characteristic is the crabbed utterance of Carlyle—

"No transaction could be handsomer on your part. . . . The money account concerns me. Please attend to that as already said. Friendliness and help cannot be paid, but money can and always should."

How warm-hearted the frank sentences of Dickens!—

"I have too great a regard for you and too high a sense of your honourable dealings to wish to depart from the custom we have already observed. Whatever price you put upon the book will satisfy me."

The author of *Lothair* wrote with equal cordiality, but in a wholly different style—

"The sympathy of a great nation is the most precious reward of authors, and an appreciation that is offered us by a foreign people has something of the character and value which we attribute to the fiat of prosperity. I accept your liberal enclosure in the spirit in which it is offered, for it comes from a gentleman whose prosperity always pleases me, and whom I respect and regard."

Here is an amusing extract from Longfellow—

"Your very generous addition to the original

sum agreed upon between us is pleasant to me, less for the sum itself than for the trait of character it reveals in you and the proof of your liberal dealing. The contingency you allude to, namely, of my employing another continental publisher, is about as remote as that of one of Dickens' characters, who bought at an auction a brass door-plate with the name of Thompson on it, thinking it possible that her daughter might marry some one of that name!"

The great publishing house familiar to every English-speaking traveller on the Continent is not to be confounded with an earlier and famous business of the same name. So early as 1796 Christopher Tauchnitz set up a printing press in Leipzig, from which later were issued the cheap and handy

> "Little Greek books with the funny type,
> They get up well at Leipzig,"

of which the rather boring Bishop Blougram speaks. These classics are still published by the million.

A nephew of this Christopher, Bernhard, Baron von Tauchnitz, was destined to be not only a great publisher, but what the late Cotter Morrison called—"A moral inventor." Born in 1816, following the trade of his uncle, he began his Continental Series in 1841, of which 2,600 had appeared in the following fifty years. Ennobled in 1860, this prince of pioneers was created one of the few Saxon life-peers in 1877. He died in 1895 surrounded by—

> "That which should accompany old age,
> As honour, love, obedience, troops of friends,"

the noble and ennobling traditions of his house being carried on by the present Baron.

II
MATILDA BETHAM
Poet, Miniature Painter, and Biographer

[*To face p.* 15

SIR WILLIAM BETHAM, ULSTER KING-AT-ARMS

II

WHAT a link with the past does the name of my aunt and godmother call up! As a child in the nursery, to have been taught to take my thumb out of my mouth and make a curtsey by a friend of Charles and Mary Lamb, by one who had collogued with the great De Staël, whose daily intercourse had been with Coleridge and the great gods of a clean century ago!

A few prefatory words concerning "the measureless Bethams," of whom Charles Lamb wrote so humorously but not always with good-humour.

There was literature in the family. Three nineteenth-century Bethams figure in the great *Dictionary of National Biography*, namely, my grandfather, the Rev. William Betham, compiler of *The Genealogical Tables of the Sovereigns of the World*, and other works still to be found on bookstalls; my uncle, Sir William Betham, Ulster King-at-Arms, whose works on Celtic archæology and in *The Parliamentary History of England* displayed much research and ingenuity; thirdly, the subject of the present memoir.

Her literary forbears, however, went much farther back.[1] *The Precepts of Warre*, "translated into Englysh" by Peter Betham, London, 1554, occurs in Lowndes' *Dictionary*. Two other literary Bethams or De Bethams are named in our great Dictionary. It was a Jesuit father of the name who accompanied James II into exile at the Court of St. Germains.

The family have ever entertained a passion for pedigrees.[2] Unfortuned in other matters, they

[1] *A House of Letters*, by Ernest Betham (great-nephew of Matilda), Jarrold & Sons, 1903–4, gives many interesting memorials of the family.

[2] The Bethams or De Bethams are an ancient Westmorland family (see Burn's *History of Westmorland* for notice of the De Bethams of Betham), and in the little church of Bethom, near Kendal, are the recumbent figures in stone of Sir Thomas de Betham and his wife, still in tolerable preservation, though dating from the reign of Richard III. For several hundred years the Bethams were baptized and buried in Morland Church, some distance to the north of Betham; and although the manor of Betham has long since passed into other hands, till lately small estates remained in the family dating from that early period. The present writer is a daughter of the little Barbara mentioned in these pages, who afterwards married

BETHAM CHURCH

[To face p. 17

have never lacked heraldic treasure. One might suppose from this cleaving to genealogy that, as in Biblical days, a bar sinister was drawn across every ungenealogical man, woman and child in the kingdom. We read (Ezra ii. 62)—" These sought their register among those that were reckoned by genealogy, but they were not found; therein were they, as polluted, put from the priesthood." [1]

Edward Edwards, of Westerfield Hall, near Ipswich, where she was born.

[1] As these lines are prepared for the press I see that the German Government has just prohibited English speech in Samoa, the island coolly handed over to Germany by the late Lord Salisbury. On a small scale this annexation was as deeply felt by the English community as Bismarck's seizure of Alsace-Lorraine by its French inhabitants. One of the earliest settlers in Stevenson's island-home, 1855, was a nephew of Sir William Betham, who no less passionately clung to his nationality than the French annexés. During the troubles of a dozen years ago, his books and the most cherished heirloom he possessed, namely, his pedigree, were destroyed by the natives. Learning that he lay hopelessly ill and that the loss greatly distressed him on his children's account, I hastily dispatched my own arbre généalogique to Apia by post. The gift reached my dying kinsman whilst he was still able mentally and bodily to rejoice in it, and amply did his message repay the loss to my-

It was a seafaring Betham who aroused Charles Lamb's ire by recounting again and again a wonderful story of a shark. " How I wish that the shark had eaten him up ! " was the humorist's regret.

The handsome, rollicking, dare-devil captain in the H.E.I.C.S. thus castigated was one of my eleven uncles and aunts, most of them in stature recalling the words—" there were giants in those days."

This much-married sailor must have possessed other fascinations besides the comeliness of Absalom. Maugre his wandering, hazardous, topsy-turvy career, he wooed and won in turn three attractive and amply dowered ladies. The scapegrace, it must be confessed, was a bit of a fortune-hunter—in the Betham pedigree, twelve centuries of record, no other delinquency stains the family annals; violent deaths many of them met, but it was by the axe on Tower Hill as victims, not by the rope at Tyburn. One noble deed covers Captain John's many lapses. A magnificent silver trophy was presented to him by a shipping company for having alone unaided

self. The document will now be doubly valuable to his descendants.

BETHAM HALL

[To face p. 18

saved one of their shipwrecked crews from drowning. Gifted with a knack of verse, he wrote and published an imitation of *Hudibras* called *Paddy Hew*. Another brother, Charles by name, migrated to what was then called Crim Tartary—what could those six or seven six-footers of a poor clergyman do at home? When examining Arthur Young's voluminous correspondence some years ago I came upon some interesting letters from this Betham, dealing with agricultural projects. What became of his schemes I do not know, but earlier I was enabled to refute the charges of parasitism and dependence made against him in Landor's *Letters*. The offensive passages were afterwards deleted.

Two younger brothers, both sailors and in the flower of their youth, perished together at sea.

The pillar of the house, the prop of his family, was Sir William Betham, a veritable " Iddo, the seer, concerning genealogies." I never saw him, or remember seeing any of my uncles, who were all middle-aged at my birth.

A high-minded man, perfect in every domestic relation, his dignified, laborious and ofttimes much-tried career is a fact to remember with pride.[1]

[1] I add from the *Times* of June 1845, the list of bibliographical curios sold after his death. What self-denial must each of his purchases imply, for he was never rich, and had a legion of claimants on his generosity.

THE BETHAM MANUSCRIPTS.—The curious and valuable collection of manuscripts collected during a long literary career by that distinguished herald, the late Sir William Betham, for many years Ulster King-of-Arms, were on Thursday last brought to the hammer at the rooms of Messrs. Sotheby and Wilkinson, and on account of their interesting nature were eagerly competed for, in most instances at extraordinarily high prices. The 198 lots produced nearly £900, and were bought chiefly by Sir Frederick Madden (for the British Museum), Dr. Neligan, Boone, Hamilton, Upham, and H. Bohn. As a specimen of the prices put upon old writings by collectors, we instance the very characteristic holograph letter of Oliver Cromwell (lot 137), addressed "For my sonn Harry Cromwell," which was secured by Mr. Monckton Milnes, M.P., for £17. Among the other curiosities we shall content ourselves by citing merely the most interesting, with their prices, *e. g.*:—Lot 7. "Archdall's Collections relating to Irish Topography," entirely in the author's autograph, £7 15s. Lot 10. "Banagher Minute Book," from 1693 to 1749, with the official signatures, secured for the Museum at £3. Lot 15. "Betham Correspondence," in 35 vols., 4to, embracing a number of notes and letters addressed to the herald by his contemporaries, a selection of which would form a readable volume, £35. Lot 17. "Betham's Abstract of the Statutes of Ireland," £10 10s. Lot 24. "Betham's List of Knights made in Ireland from 1565 to 1839, with paintings of their arms," £8 15s.

Sir William had never, I believe, studied at a
university. As each of his works on archæology

Lot 25. "Betham's Inrollment of Matters relating to the
Counties Palatine in Ireland," £8. Lot 26. "Betham's
List of ancient Historical Documents relating to Ireland,"
£13 13s. Lot 30. "Boyle Papers," relating to the con-
spiracy in 1598, when Mr. Boyle, afterwards the great
Earl of Cork, was thrown into prison, charged with
"felony, perjury, forgery, and other crimes," £6 6s.
Lot 33. "Brooks's (York Herald) Heraldic Commonplace
Book" entirely in his autograph, and containing among
other curious entries a complaint of the injustice of Mr.
Secretary Cecil making "Westminster skolemaster one
William Camden Clarenceux King of Arms over the heads
of the old officers," £17. Lot 43. "Concilium Generale"
(the 4th Lateran, in which the Albigenses were condemned)
written in the 14th century by an English scribe, £10.
Lot 46. Sir R. Cox's "Description of Corke," in his own
handwriting, £11 11s. Lot 52. "Dinn-Seanchus-Erenn"
—a transcript of this celebrated Irish topography, in the
handwriting of Professor Connellan, £17. Lot 53.
"Domesday Boke of Dyvelyn Citie (Dublin)," transcript
by Sir W. Betham, £19. Lot 54. "Dublin Castle State
Letter Book in 1782," probably, as was formerly the
custom, disposed of as a perquisite, but now redeemed for
£5 15s. Lot 64. "Fulberti Episcopi Carnotensis Opus-
cula," written in the 14th century, £5. Lot 71. "Holt,
the Irish Rebel Commander-in-Chief's, Autobiography,"
in his own handwriting, £4 10s. Lot 73. "Horæ B.
Mariæ Virginis," with seven illuminations, £25 10s.
Lot 75. "Collectanea de Rebus Hibernicis," 1173-1600, a
transcript, £16 16s. Lot 77. "Annals of Ireland," from
1559 to 1686 inclusive, £8 8s. Lot 79. "Liber Regalis
Visitationis in tribus Provinciis Hiberniæ," being the fair

appeared, the dons endeavoured to write him down. Undaunted by sneers, unruffled by attacks, he pursued his way, leaving behind a record much more precious than the pedigree dating from Alfred the Great by which his Samoan nephew set such store!

Matilda Betham, his senior by a year or two, was in her prime when receiving the accompanying letters—

---

copy of the Commissioners' Report, a document of national importance, and which was secured for the nation by Sir F. Madden for £31. Lots 80 to 87. "The Original Entries of Recognizances in the Irish Chancery," etc., were purchased by Mr. Boone for £38. Lot 88. "Original MS. of the Orders in Council for Irish Affairs during the Protectorate," Sir F. Madden secured for £6 6s. Lot 118. "Lodge's Historical Collections for Ireland," transcribed from the originals, for which the Government gave his widow an annuity of £500 for life, was purchased by Mr. Boone for £151. Lot 138. "Servyce of the Holy Trynyte," an English MS. of the 15th century, £10. Lot 140. "O'Reilly's Irish-English Dictionary," with numerous MS. additions by Professor Connellan, £29. Lot 158. "Poems," in the autograph of Payne Fisher, Poet Laureat to Oliver Cromwell, £3. Lot 162. "Quarles's Divine Fancies," in the poet's autograph, £5 10s. Lot 167. "Rogeri de Waltham Compendium Morale," MS. of the 14th century on vellum, £27. Lot 168. "Bishop Rooth's Analecta Sacra," in English, £7 15s. Lot 180. "Dean Swift's Humorous Poems," in his own autograph, unpublished, £10 10s.

"I return you by a careful hand the MSS.," wrote Charles Lamb. "Did I not ever love your verses? The domestic half will be a sweet heirloom to have in the family. 'Tis fragrant with cordiality. What friends you must have had or dreamed of having! and what a widow's cruse of heartiness you have doled among them!" "I remember," wrote Southey to her in 1815, "that I did not say half as much about your poem as I ought to have done; but this shall be made amends for in proper place, for I like it so much that it will give me very sincere pleasure to say how good it is in a manner that may be serviceable." From Allan Cunningham came the following enthusiastic eulogium of the same work, *The Lay of Marie:* "How could you suspect my admiration and love of poetry by apologising for gratifying me with the perusal of a poem so full of fine feeling and fancy, beautiful description and imagery, impressive morality, and melting pathos?"

Posterity did not endorse the poet's verdict; the name of Matilda Betham only recalls one who was a "strong-minded woman" when to be thus named implied singularity, and who enjoyed the conversancy and friendship of the immortal brother and sister, Charles and Mary Lamb.

"Many people have thought me naturally a singular and perhaps imprudent person because I rhymed and ventured into the world as an artist," she wrote; "but I belonged to a large family, and dreaded dependence. My mother's handsome [1] fortune was lessened by the expense of a Chancery suit of eleven years' standing. My father's hopes of preferment were one by one disappointed by death and translation of bishops, and once by having delayed a request because he would not call about it on a Sunday. The destination of his children, therefore, became modified by existing circumstances. In my visits to London I had learned French. The desire of knowing Italian had been kindled by reading Hoole's *Metastasio*, and I took advantage of an invitation to Cambridge to have a half-year's instruction from Agostino Isola, a delightful old man, who had been the preceptor of Gray the poet, Pitt, and others."

[1] Handsome in those days and under those circumstances. The daughter of a French merchant, a Huguenot refugee, her dowry was £1000.

She studied, or rather taught herself, miniature-painting, with a view to making it a profession, and had so much talent that her first efforts were hailed as full of promise. But there were no art-schools for women, nothing to be had in the way of thorough teaching; and charming as many of these likenesses are, they often betray both inaccuracy of drawing and faulty technique.

Her friends one and all encouraged such literary and artistic aspirations. "I tell you," said one, "for the thousandth time, that you are full of genius; several paths to fame lie open to you, and if you don't contrive to march through one of them, you deserve to have your mental feet cut off." The writer of these enthusiastic lines, Lady Bedingfield, was an early friend, and their affection for each other lasted till old age, when she wrote, "You took me for better and for worse, dear Matilda, fifty years ago." Lady Bedingfield was the daughter of Sir C. Jerningham of Cossy, afterwards wife of Sir Richard Bedingfield, and later became one of the ladies in waiting at Court. This large-hearted and gifted woman, whose charming nature bespeaks itself in every line of her long correspondence with Matilda Betham, was said herself to be a born artist. Sir Joshua Reynolds remarked when looking at her sketches, "It is a pity she cannot be brought up as an artist." But in those days to do more than toy with art or literature was not considered becoming in ladies of position, and in her early letters she says of herself, "I feel something within me, certain latent powers, that, had my destiny left me as you are, single and independent of control, would, I think, have made me enter the lists of fame in the painting way; but situated as I am, my imagination works, but I have no time or opportunity to acquire that method and precision of design which, though the inferior part of the art, are nevertheless necessary to our defence, if once we outstep the privacy of a family or friendly circle and expose ourselves to the cold criticism of the public." Lady Bedingfield's letters are delightful compositions, alike those written in girlhood, middle life, and old age. They were published a few years ago.

Matilda went to London and had a brief, brilliant period of literary and artistic success. She wrote a *Biographical Dictionary of Celebrated Women*, the first of its kind—truly the work of a pioneer—a work of much usefulness in its day, and compiled with considerable taste and care. Her pictures were exhibited at Somerset House, and, besides portrait painting, she found time to contribute poetical pieces to the *Monthly* and other magazines. She also gave Shakespearean readings. It was at this time that her friendship commenced with celebrated contemporaries. She visited the Southeys at Keswick, the celebrated Ladies of Llangollen in Wales, Mrs. Schimmelpenninck at Bath, and was constantly a guest of the Barbaulds at Stoke Newington, and the Lambs in the Temple. She met Madame de Staël, and was much struck with the fine eyes and audacious vanity of that great woman. Each day of this happy time in London was marked by some pleasant event, as the following entries in her diary testify: "Supped with the Lambs." "Spent the evening with the Barbaulds." "At the Lambs', and with them to the play." "Had a party, Mr. and Mrs. Lamb, Mr. Hazlitt," etc. "Dined with Barbara at the Lambs'." The Barbara in question was her youngest sister, as I have said, my mother (afterwards Mrs. Edwards), to whom Mary Lamb wrote one of the most charming letters ever written to a child—here given—

Letter from Mary Lamb to Barbara Betham
(aged 14)

"Nov. 2, 1814.

"It is very long since I have met with such an agreeable surprise as the sight of your letter, my kind young friend, afforded me. Such a nice letter as it is too; and what a pretty hand you write! I congratulate you on this attainment with great pleasure, because I have so often felt the disadvantage of my own wretched hand-writing.

"You wish for London news. I rely upon your sister Ann for gratifying you in this respect, yet I have been endeavouring to recollect whom you might have seen here, and what may have happened to them since, and this effort has only brought the image of little Barbara Betham, unconnected with any other person, so strongly before my eyes, that I seem as if I had no other subject to write upon. Now, I think I see you with your feet propped upon the fender, your two hands spread out upon your knees—an attitude you always chose when we were in familiar confidential conversation together—telling me long stories of your own home, where now you say you are 'moping on with the same thing every day,' and which then presented nothing but pleasant recollections to your mind. How well I remember your quiet, steady face bent over your book. One day, conscience-stricken at having wasted so much of your precious time in reading, and feeling yourself, as you prettily said, 'quite useless to me,' you went to my drawers and hunted out some unhemmed pocket-handkerchiefs, and by no means could I prevail upon you to resume your story-books till you had hemmed them all. I remember, too, your teaching my little maid to read, your sitting with her a whole evening to console her for the death of her sister, and that she in her turn endeavoured to become a comforter to you, the next evening, when you wept at the sight of Mrs. Holcroft, from whose school you had recently eloped because you were not partial to sitting in the stocks. Those tears, and a few you once dropped when my brother teased you about your supposed fondness for an apple-dumpling, were the only interruptions to the calm contentedness of your unclouded brow.

"We still remain the same as you left us, neither taller, nor wiser, nor perceptibly older, but three years must have made a great alteration in you. How very much, dear Barbara, I should like to see you!

"We still live in Temple Lane, but I am now sitting in a room you never saw. Soon after you left us we were distressed by the cries of a cat, which seemed to proceed from the garrets adjoining ours, and only separated from ours by a locked door on the farther side of my brother's bedroom, which you know was the little room at the top of the kitchen stairs. We had the lock forced, and let poor puss out from behind a panel of the wainscot, and she lived with us from that time, for we were in gratitude bound to keep her, as she had introduced us to four untenanted, unowned rooms, and by degrees we have taken possession of these unclaimed apartments, first putting up lines to dry our clothes, then moving my brother's bed into one of these more commodious than his own rooms; and last winter, my brother being unable to pursue a work he had begun owing to the kind interruptions of friends who were more at leisure than himself, I persuaded him that he might write at ease in one of these rooms, as he could not then hear the door knock, or hear himself denied to be at home, which was sure to make him call out and convict the poor maid in a fib. Here, I said, he might be almost really not at home. So I put in an old grate, and made him a fire in the largest of these garrets and carried in his own table and one chair, and bid him write away and consider himself as much alone as if he were in a lodging in the midst of Salisbury Plain, or any other wide, unfrequented place, where he could expect few visitors to break in upon his solitude. I left him quite delighted with his new acquisition, but in a few hours he came down again with a sadly dismal face. He could do nothing, he said, with those bare, whitewashed walls before his eyes. He could not write in that dull, unfurnished prison!

" The next day, before he came home from his office, I had gathered up various bits of old carpeting to cover the floor, and to a little break the blank look of the bare walls, I hung up a few old prints that used to ornament the kitchen; and after dinner, with great boast of what improvement I had made, I took Charles once more into

31

his new study. A week of busy labours followed, in which I think you would not have disliked to be our assistant; my brother and I almost covered the walls with prints, for which purpose he cut out every print from every book in his old library, coming in every now and then to ask my leave to strip a fresh poor author, which he might not do, you know, without my permission, as I am elder sister. There was such pasting, such consultation upon these portraits, and where the series of pictures from Ovid,[1] Milton, and Shakespeare would show to most advantage, and in what obscure corner authors of humble rank should be allowed to tell their stories. All the books gave up their stories but one, a translation from Ariosto, with a delicious set of four-and-twenty prints, and for which I had marked out a conspicuous place; when lo, we found at the moment the scissors were going to work, that a part of the poem was printed at the back of every picture! What a cruel disappointment! To conclude this long story about nothing, the poor despised garret

[1] This Ovid, denuded of pictures, was presented by Mary Lamb to Matilda Betham, and is in the author's possession.

is now called the print-room, and is become our most familiar sitting-room.

"The lions still live in Exeter Change. Returning home through the Strand, I often hear them roar about twelve o'clock at night. I never hear them without thinking of you, because you seemed so pleased with the sight of them, and said your young companions would stare when you told them you had seen a lion.

"And now, my dear Barbara, farewell. I have not written such a long letter a long time, but I am very sorry I had nothing amusing to write about. Wishing you may pass happily through the rest of your school days, and every future day of your life,

> "I remain,
>> "Your affectionate friend,
>>> "M. LAMB.

"My brother sends his love to you. You say you are not so tall as Louisa—you must be; you cannot so degenerate from the rest of your family.

"Now you have begun I shall hope to have the pleasure of hearing from you again. I shall always receive a letter from you with very great delight."

The following letter addressed by Charles Lamb to Mary Betham concerned a small legacy left to his sister by Anne Norman (*née* Betham). It was communicated to the *Academy* some years ago by Amelia Blandford Edwards, to whom I had presented it as a precious relic. Amelia, my senior, added a charming recollection of Matilda as known by her in her later years.

"Lamb's letter," she wrote, "is curiously illustrative of the warmth, impulsiveness, and irresolution of the writer. Touched even to tears, he begins by disclaiming the legacy. At first he will none of it—'not a penny.' Next he proposes to 'halve it' with Matilda, who was the least prosperous of her family. Lastly, as the ink cools in his pen, he proposes that his sister and he shall share it with Matilda in three equal parts. The letter occupies the first page of a sheet of foolscap. Had he written a few more lines and turned the leaf, he would probably have ended by taking the whole.

"'Dear Mary Betham, I remember you all, and tears come out when I think on the years that have separated us. That dear Anne should so long have remember'd us affects me. My dear Mary, my poor sister is not, nor will be for two months perhaps, capable of appreciating the *kind old long memory* of dear Anne.

"'But not a penny will I take, and I can answer for my Mary when she recovers, if the sum left can contribute in any way to the comfort of Matilda.

"'We will halve it, or we will take a bit of it, as a token, rather than wrong her. So pray consider it as an amicable arrangement. I write in great haste, or you won't get it before you go.

"'*We do not want the money;* but if dear Matilda does not much want it, why, we will take our thirds. God bless you.

"'C. LAMB.

"'I am not at Enfield, but at Mr. Walden's, Church Street, Edmonton, Middlesex.'

"The letter is not dated, but bears postmark of June 5, 1833. It is addressed to 'Miss Mary Betham, 27 King Street, Cheapside; or to the care of Sir Wm. Betham, Dublin.'

"My own recollection of Matilda Betham," wrote Amelia, "is particularly vivid. When I was a very young girl, she used to drop in occasionally to my mother's tea-table on a summer evening, and charm us with talk about Madame de Staël, Coleridge, Southey, and the days of the great French Revolution. She lodged at that time, I think, in Lamb's Conduit Street, which she liked for its proximity to the British Museum, where she was a constant student in the old Reading Rooms of dismal memory. She generally carried a big basket and a Brobdingnag umbrella. From the depths of this basket (which, besides the writing materials she had been using at the Museum, contained her cap and all kinds of miscellaneous marketings) she would sometimes bring out some magazine of many years gone by, and read aloud, with not ungraceful emphasis, a poem of her own. She had a large, round, jovial face, bright blue eyes, a mobile mouth, and somewhat short grey hair, which strayed from under her cap all round her neck 'in silvery slips,' like a man's.

"In fact, she was not unlike the portraits of Coleridge. Her eccentricities of dress were proverbial. My father once met her in a frequented London thoroughfare, serenely walking in crimson velvet slippers, and followed by a train of little ragamuffins, to whose 'chaff' she was good-humouredly indifferent."

From earliest childhood I received notes from my godmother, and those letters, written microscopically on odd fragments of paper, were always about books and authors. She could rarely, if ever, bring herself to condemn a work, so dearly did she love all books, but she never tired of admiring the best. She wrote to her eight-year-old godchild of Dryden, Pope, Addison, and chatted of the great writers, her contemporaries and friends. Her mind was saturated with literature, and she very early imbued her namesake with the same taste. My first recollection of her is vivid, despite the long interval of years, for I was a mere child when she died. She was a ready wit, and nothing—neither narrow means, checks, literary disappointments, nor the infirmities of age —could embitter that smooth temper, nor subdue those cheerful spirits. Bless her memory! The heedless child who did not even preserve those letters she was at such pains to write in her old age could, as she reached maturity, realise the service thus rendered to her and the good seed thus sown in her mind.

Her declining years were spent in London. At Henry Robinson's and other literary gatherings the oddly-dressed old woman, who was wont to enter leaning on a stick, her face beaming with animation and intelligence, was usually surrounded by a little court. "I would rather talk to Matilda Betham than to the most beautiful young woman in the world," said one of her youthful admirers of the other sex at this time.[1] Those who listened to her bright sallies, her piquant stories, her apt quotations, forgot the oddness of dress and appearance. From her father, who lived to be ninety-two, and possessed his faculties unclouded to the last, she seems to have inherited her humour. Almost the last words he uttered were a pun. He was walking up and down the room, leaning on his youngest daughter's arm the day before he died, and said, smiling, "I am walking slowly, yet I am going fast." "The wise must die as well as the foolish, and I won't be poisoned," said Matilda Betham in her declining years, and no persuasion or entreaty could ever induce her to touch physic.

[1] This gallant remark is paralleled in the first and delightful volume of Disraeli's life, just out. Writing of an aged lady met at Gibraltar, the youth, for he was no more, says: "You would think you were charming away the hour with a blooming beauty of Mayfair."

Matilda Betham

She died in 1852, and was buried at Highgate Cemetery.

Like the romantic poetry of Miss Landon, and, later, the Hon. Mrs. Norton, the *Lay of Marie* belonged to a fashion which was destined to pass away; but some of her smaller pieces possess a touching grace and pathos deserving of a better fate; the following, for instance, which has been translated into German.

"How solemn is the sick man's room
  To friends or kindred lingering near,
Poring on the uncertain gloom
  In silent heaviness and fear!

How sad, his feeble hand in thine,
  The start of every pulse to share;
With painful haste each wish divine,
  Yet feel the hopelessness of care!

To turn aside the full fraught eye,
  Lest those faint orbs perceive the tear;
To bear the weight of every sigh,
  Lest it should reach that wakeful ear!

In the dread stillness of the night,
  To lose the faint, faint sound of breath;
To listen in restrain'd affright,
  To deprecate each thought of death!

And, when a movement chased that fear,
  And gave thy heart's blood leave to flow,
In thrilling awe the prayer to hear,
  Through the closed curtain murmur'd low;

The prayer of him whose holy tongue
  Had never yet exceeded truth;
Upon whose guardian care has hung
  The whole dependence of thy youth;

Who, noble, dauntless, frank, and mild,
  Was, for his very goodness, fear'd;
Beloved with fondness like a child,
  And like a blessed saint revered.

I have known friends, but who can feel
  The kindness such a father knew!
I served him still with tender zeal,
  But knew not then how much was due!"

Some years ago her pretty song, "Manuel, I do not shed a tear," translated into Latin and published by an academic journal, was forwarded to me by an anonymous correspondent. How happy would such a compliment have rendered the author!

But Matilda Betham knew neither envy nor repining. The common things of life did not at all trouble her. One day a caller found her lunching, rather dining, at mid-day, off a fried herring and a pineapple, offering of some opulent friend! The complacency with which she was sitting down to both gave the key to her character. Both the herrings and pineapples of life, figuratively speaking, were taken as matters of course.

III

AMELIA BLANDFORD EDWARDS

Egyptologist, Novelist, Artist, Musician

[To face p. 43

WESTERFIELD HALL

III

FRESH in my mind as if it happened yesterday is the recollection of our first meeting in my childhood's home, Westerfield Hall, Ipswich— herself just entering her teens, the country cousin, a child in the nursery. Visits from uncles and aunts were great occasions at that time, and always prepared for by a grand baking of cakes, rusks and apple turnovers; the family silver and china would be got out, and besides tea of the strongest and best served with cream, old harvest beer, clear as sherry and twice as strong, ham pickled at home after elaborate Suffolk fashion in strong home-brewed, spice and sugar, potted meats—of course home-made also—and other dainties, light and substantial, regaled the guests. "Next moon," or "the moon after next," was the way in which invitations were given and accepted. When folks had to drive ten or twelve miles

43

across country, often through fields and lanes, they paid visits either in the longest days of the year or when the moon was at the full.

As it happened, the younger Westerfield children, of whom I was one, had no Suffolk cousins nearly of their own age; the aunts and uncles who came to tea in gigs were bachelors and maiden ladies. All the more exciting, therefore, was the prospect of seeing this one, now on a holiday visit with father and mother.

Visitors arrived early, about three or four o'clock in the afternoon, so as to afford the uncles time for a stroll round the farm. Upon this occasion the party came later, and we could only guess what the Londoner was like till after tea; she, of course, with our elder sisters, taking hers in the " best parlour "—drawing-room and dining-room were unheard-of names in those days. The family lived and took meals in what was called " the keeping room." The nursery governess of my childhood did not possess the acquirements now obligatory. Reading, writing, arithmetic and a smattering of French was all I got from teachers at Westerfield. But good nature all these threw into the bargain, and I well remember how the

[*To face p.* 45

WESTERFIELD CHURCH AND RECTORY

tedium of waiting for our eagerly expected visitor was beguiled by stories. At last we heard voices on the stairs, three little pinafored figures jumped excitedly from their high chairs, the door flew open, and there she stood—a tall girl of twelve or thirteen, with regular features, pale, clear-complexioned, and abundance of dark-brown hair tied in a pigtail down her back. In highest spirits, the personification of fun and childish daring, she surveyed her three little close-cropped cousins, and then, turning to those of her own age who accompanied her, pounced upon half a loaf of bread, remainder of the nursery tea.

"Who dares me to throw this out of the window?" she cried, undauntedly meeting our aghast gaze. Before the governess could remonstrate, my second sister had taken up the challenge, and lo! away went the bread into the shrubbery below, exactly opposite the best parlour window!

What happened after that little escapade I do not remember, the incident taking hold of my youthful imagination. I was also much struck by the clear enunciation and quick, ready speech, even educated folks in Suffolk being apt to imbibe the dialect—that dragging sing-song, so difficult to get rid of in after life. It has been said that one Suffolker can recognise another even from a word or two uttered on the top of a London omnibus. Be this as it may, Amelia's correct, careful English characterised her at this early period, and next to the pigtail and the throwing of the bread out of the window, constituted my earliest impressions.

Her parents were figures not to be forgotten by a child, either: the spare, upright Peninsular officer, taciturn yet not uncheerful, exact to punctiliousness, the soul of probity and honour; and his clever, lively Irish wife. From her father, Amelia inherited those businesslike qualities so handsomely acknowledged by an editor of the *Academy*—

"Miss Edwards was in truth a model contributor—never declining a request, punctual to her promises, writing in a clear, bold hand, and considerate of the convenience of printer as well as editor."

I dare aver that my uncle was never a second late for anything in his life. He became, indeed, almost automatic by this habit of perpetually regarding the clock; and perhaps punctuality carried to excess cost his daughter her life. When lecturing in America, rather than break an engagement, she gave a lecture immediately after an accident to her wrist, and as soon as this was over, travelled several hundred miles in order to deliver another next day. Her health declined from that date.

But a stern, unflinching sense of duty was not the paramount characteristic of the old soldier, by reason of health at fifty condemned to a civilian's life. When the Crimean War broke out, although verging on threescore and ten, he sent in his name to the War Office as "able and willing to serve." The sound of the trumpet had stirred his blood. He would fain have donned sword and tunic. His miniature and Peninsular medal won at Coruña had ever the place of honour in his daughter's study.

The paternal pedigree, if homely, was no despicable one. I shall take the reader by and by to the fine old church of Gosbeck, where, amid wildflowers and grass, stand the handsome tombs of Thomas and Margaret Edwards, parents of the numerous family of whom Amelia's father came, I believe, third. The Edwardses are as numerous in Suffolk as the Joneses in Wales. Our grandparents belonged to the class later on, but never in their own time, called "gentlemen farmers," *i. e.* occupiers of land on a large scale which they rented.

On the maternal side she inherited more brilliant gifts, wit, great versatility, rapid powers of acquirement and expression, also the perilous dower of personal fascination. No one ever exercised stronger influence, and it was hardly her fault if at times she awakened interest or affection she could not return. From her mother also came practical qualities. The highly complexioned, bright-eyed, large-featured, little Irishwoman—descendant of the Walpoles—although accomplished, as the word accomplishment was then understood, possessed talents invaluable to the wife of an officer living on half pay. She was a skilled housewife, and extraordinarily clever in making the most of small means. As if prescient of her only child's literary distinction, she forbore to give her the domestic training she had herself received. The first woman Egyptologist never threaded a needle or made a cup of tea in her life. She certainly never confected an apple-pudding, although she would not have puzzled her brains as did George the Third concerning the deep mystery enveloping the business.

I may here mention that the London cousin had already attained a literary reputation. When only nine years old, she had seen in a penny journal the announcement of a prize offered for the best temperance story. Fired with ambition, the authoress in pinafore set secretly to work, and to her own intense delight and the far intenser pride of her parents, carried off the palm. Throughout these early years till she attained womanhood, her principal teacher was her mother. Little—except in the matter of music—she ever owed to schools and professors. She always said that she could teach herself any subject better than learn it of others.

Neither at Creeting nor Baylham, her holiday resorts in Suffolk, had the youthful visitor companions of her own age. Few children, perhaps, ever lived less with children. At home in London she was her mother's constant companion, whilst on these country visits she was the pride, the wonder, and, I may add, the terror, of bachelor uncles and maiden aunts. From her love of escapade they never knew what to expect, and the more she tormented the more adorable she became. Upon one occasion she turned the tap of a cask of old harvest beer, and when the trick was discovered, half the contents had run out. At another time she locked up a somewhat precise, elderly aunt for hours in the pantry. These freaks were overlooked on account of the phenomenal acquirements of their niece. A child who had gained the prize for a story at nine years of age could hardly be expected to behave as others! As we shall see, her exploits were not all of a disturbing nature. One at least is noteworthy among recorded juvenile achievements.

Creeting St. Peter's, one Creeting of a group, is about a mile and a half from Needham Market, cleanest, neatest of the many neat, clean towns of Suffolk. You might, in local phraseology, eat off the pavements of that town. The one long winding street is by no means monotonous; beautiful old timbered houses with white or pinkish walls, gables and carol windows break the uniformity, and very striking is the fine old church in dark grey stone.

A STREET IN NEEDHAM MARKET

[To face p. 5

Amelia Blandford Edwards

Needham Market no longer possessing a market, and therefore generally called Needham, is, I should say, little changed from those early days. The principal modern building is the handsome railway station fronting the Swan Inn, formerly posting-house, bicycling head-quarters at the present time. It is a delightful old inn, and, except for paper and paint, must be just what it was when the London coach set down the little three-year-old Amelia and her parents; for she had paid several visits to Suffolk before the meeting described above. Both inside and out, the place recalls the past. You lose your way in the numerous passages, coming now upon a low-roofed, wainscoted parlour, now upon an enormous room used as a ballroom by Georgian beaux and beauties. The house fronts the quiet street, but close behind where the stableyard ends, the country begins. You can gather cowslips, marsh marigolds and wild roses within a stone's throw of your modest but cosy quarters; landlord and landlady welcoming you as a friend, yourself no mere number but a personality, an individual. Such at least was the case twenty years ago.

Passing under the railway arch on the road to Creeting, we obtain a sweet view of the sleepy old-world townling; it rises above the meadows, the little river Gipping winding by pollard willows towards Stowmarket, on either side pastures bright with cowslips, wood anemones and ladysmocks, the whole rustic and pastoral as well can be. That delicious path reaches from Stowmarket to Ipswich—no prettier twelve-mile walk in eastern England. No sooner are we out of Needham Market than we are in Creeting— and what a new world here for the quick eyes of the little Londoner! Even in 1892 the place seemed to me rusticity itself, hardly changed, indeed, from the Creeting of my childhood. The road lies amidst cornfields, in the month of May emerald green, and stretches of brown fallow, here and there a neat thatched cottage with white-washed walls breaking the solitude.

The farm-houses hereabouts are all of a pattern, brown-roofed, white-walled, at some distance from the road, yet fronting it, as if the builders wished to give a peep of the outside world. There is no attempt at picturesqueness or effect. On either side are farm buildings and horsepond,

HILL FARM, CREETING ST. PETER'S

[To face p. 53

flower garden and orchard being out of sight, the whole, indeed, of unpoetic appearance. But when was the country unpoetic to a happy, petted, urban child? We can fancy the large-eyed Amy—as she was called later, although the name was unsuited to her strong character—being lifted out of Uncle William's gig, and taking in everything, the kitchen, spacious, spick and span, from the roof hanging home-cured hams pickled in old harvest beer and spice, the frothing milk-pails being brought in from the dairy, the "keeping room" with its appetising board, everything of the best and everything home-made, the greatest novelty of all being the jug of harvest beer and goblets, invariable adjuncts of the farm-house tea-table.

There were a few books stowed away in cupboards—*Clarissa Harlowe* I remember ferreting out among others when I was twelve years old. But more attractive than any library was the old-fashioned garden at the back of the house. Here I found nothing changed except that a few trees have been planted. From the walled-in fruit and vegetable garden with its borders of box we pass into the orchard she loved so well, in which, perhaps, the happiest hours of her happy childhood were spent. At the time of my visit above-named the fruit trees showed delicate white and pink blossom, and the long, damp grass was dotted with cowslips; but in those summer holidays, mother and daughter would almost live out of doors, some cool spot of orchard or garden being chosen, and diversion never wanting; the harvest field, the duck-pond, the poultry yard close by, rustic sights and sounds, making the London home seem far off and dreamlike. When wet weather drove the happy holiday-makers indoors, there was yet distraction enough and to spare. The author of *Pharaohs, Fellahs and Explorers* never received a lesson in drawing, except from her mother, till she visited Rome years later. That she possessed a very remarkable talent for drawing the accompanying illustration will show.

Leading out of the best bedchamber (bedroom it was never called in those days) is a bare, whitewashed cupboard with a window, and which was used as a box-room, in winter as an apple-chamber. During one of Amelia's visits, she set to work upon what seemed a presumptuous under-

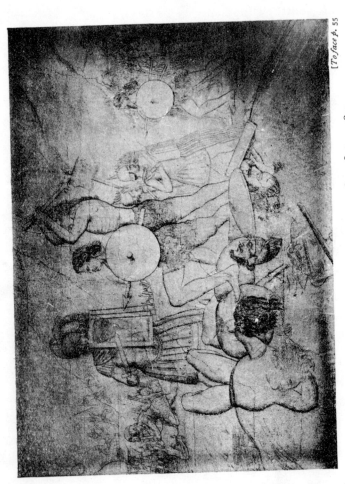

THE CARTOON IN THE APPLE-CHAMBER, *circa* 1843 or 1844.

taking. This was nothing less than a cartoon of her own design in black chalk, that should cover the centre wall, a space of two yards in length and rather less in height—the subject, " The Landing of the Romans in Britain." True enough, to the wonderment of uncles and aunts, neighbours and serving-folk, the figures grew one by one, that of Julius Cæsar being the most prominent, till the whole was completed. Such a feat would naturally spread the fame of the youthful artist far and wide, and would not soon be forgotten by younger cousins. The cartoon remained throughout life as clearly impressed on my memory as if seen but yesterday. And to my amusement, when revisiting the place after an absence of more than a quarter of a century— I had not seen the apple-chamber since my girl-hood—I found the design almost intact. Time alone had effaced a line here and there. No whitewasher had been permitted to touch the wall. And almost intact it remains to this day, the accompanying photograph dating from February of this year!

Creeting St. Peter's was the home of her Uncle William and Aunt Maria; but Baylham, home of our Uncle Henry and Aunt Betsy, was a holiday resort loved no less. The annual visit was divided between both farm-houses, Baylham being by far the more poetic of the two.

If Creeting is rusticity itself, what should be said of Baylham? Here and there through the trees peep whitewashed, thatched cottages with little flower-gardens and bee-hives, the broad expanse of cornland and pasture set round with lofty hedges, stately old elms, and pollard oaks, winding lanes and banks starred with wild flowers—such is the landscape that welcomes the traveller now, and such it was in Amelia's childhood. A wondrous sense of peace, pastoralness and permanence takes possession of us amid these scenes. No spot throughout the length and breadth of England surely had been less changed within half a century.

Lane upon lane we passed, farm-house upon farm-house, each with barns and duck-pond; yet it seemed as if we should never reach the especial one we were in quest of. My own recollections dated from my twelfth year, my companion's from his fifth, for a cousin still living in those parts had kindly acted as cicerone. Soon we

[To face p. 57

A COTTAGE, BAYLHAM, 1892

came in sight of a grey-towered church crowning a hill, and both of us exclaimed, " Then the farmhouse must be close by." We so well remembered the hot walk to church on Sunday mornings. To shorten the road, our driver, whose notions were of the vaguest, had turned into a cartway leading from field to field, just bright with cowslip and lady-smock, many a wayside pool " flaunting its marigold." Past snug, old-world farmsteads we strolled, each, as it seemed, at the world's end, and again and again I said, " Here we are."

My companion, however, had clearly impressed on his memory one feature which as yet I had not identified. This was a large, wide pond that made a curve at one end touching the road, the outer edge lost amid the overarching apple-trees of the orchard. At last the right farm was found, and slowly, bit by bit, the once familiar place came back to me. Most picturesque is the aspect from the road, although the fascination to a childish mind would lie beyond. All the rusticity of Creeting, with a touch of added charm, are here. You step out of the front door to find yourself in a little old-fashioned flower garden, bee-hives placed under the thick hedges. Leading out of this, green paths wind about the beautiful piece of water, the low boughs of apple and pear-trees making you stoop at every turn. That wide, clear pond with its reflections, grassy banks, shifting lights and shadows, we may be sure, was a favourite haunt of the Londoners, perhaps to Amelia even afforded a first vivid impression of natural beauty. And close by, whenever mother and daughter felt inclined for a stroll, lay scenes equally sweet and rustic, by-paths through the rustling corn that led to the church on the hill, little larch woods, bright as emerald under the blue sky, thatched cottages with deep roofs and flower gardens. Again and again in the midst of absorbing interests and occupations, she yearned for a sight of Suffolk. Not many years ago we projected a little journey that should be devoted to reminiscences of our early life; but time and opportunity were wanting to both.

I have mentioned that our paternal grand-parents are buried at Gosbeck, and this also was to have formed a feature of our pilgrimage. No one ever set more store by lineage than Amelia. She rejoiced in her descent on her mother's side from the illustrious family of Walpole, and anything she could learn of the more modest paternal ancestry interested her extremely. It was not very much.

It is a beautiful drive from Needham Market to Gosbeck, interesting alike to archæologist and artist. By Bosmere, with its lovely little lake, surrounded by meadows and pollard elms, we reached Coddenham, as pretty a village as England can show. It is indeed a gem of gems; its picturesque houses, alike mansion and cottage, set in pretty gardens or richly wooded grounds, are gracefully grouped around the church, here as elsewhere in Suffolk placed on a hill, or rather hillock, hills in my native county being unknown. The church itself, which, fortunately, is always open, has a very fine stone roof and a quite remarkable interior; the ceiling of old carved timber, the ancient marbles and brasses, the curious bas-relief of the vestry—all these are well worth a visit. Few country churches have more to show alike within and without. Pretty thatched cottages, clean and trim as Swiss châlets, fine old manor houses with richly-wooded grounds, lie on the farther side of the church; but as we approach

Gosbeck the scenery changes. The road now winds amid level fields and meadows, nothing to break the monotony, the chill east wind blowing keenly across the plain.

Gosbeck church stands on one of the coldest sites in this part of England. As we climbed the wind-tossed, cowslip-dotted slope, the easterly blast blew piercingly; what must church-going here be in winter, seeing that in the last few days of April we longed for furs, the warm winter wraps left behind? However, we battled with the wind manfully; a young niece who accompanied us gathering cowslips with happy unconcern, whilst we inspected the moss-covered, weather-stained tombs of Amelia's grandparents and my own. A group of Edwards' gravestones are clustered here, conspicuous among these the solid, roofed-in tombs of Thomas Edwards and Margaret his wife, the former buried in 1816, the latter a little later. Margaret Dove came of highly respectable Suffolk stock, and bore her husband a numerous family of sons and daughters, Amelia's father being one of the elder children.

As we continue our drive, we catch sight of a

large farm-house, just visible above the trees on our left, and this was the home of my cousin's father and my own.[1]

Taking a homeward route by way of Hemingstone, we find ourselves once more amid charming scenery. Hemingstone Hall is one of the fine old mansions for which Suffolk is famous, and the country round about is delightful. Magnificent old trees, oak and elm, stud beautiful park-like sweeps, sweet cottages peep from bowers of honeysuckle and wild rose, rich woods crown the rising ground here and there. And again we come upon the Gipping, a broad bright belt of blue winding amid the green.

Creeting and Baylham were holiday haunts, revisited in summer time only, associated with youthful pranks, delightsome days and also clinging affections. It was, above all, her Aunt Maria to whom the little girl clung fondly, a somewhat prim but warm-hearted maiden lady never wholly lost sight of. But Amelia's home was in London, a part of London, moreover, as unfamiliar to most

---

[1] Close to Gosbeck lies Stonham Aspall, for many years home of my grandfather, the Rev. W. Betham. (See "Matilda Betham.")

people as remote corners of Africa. Half a century ago Pentonville was by no means deemed uninhabitable. Islington possessed suburban charm. To live within a stone's throw of the Angel or Eagle might sound old-fashioned, that was all. Amelia's first home, and, I believe, birthplace, was No. 1 Westmoreland Place, City Road. The situation suited her father, who, having retired from the army in consequence of ill-health, had procured a post in a city branch of the London and Westminster Bank. Later, a much pleasanter house was taken in Wharton Street, Percy Circus. But my first acquaintance with my cousin's London life began at Westmoreland Place.

Mrs. Edwards must have been more than mortal had she concealed her pride in her darling. The achievements of the youthful story-teller, artist, musician and very clever actress, were freely vaunted in her presence. It would hardly have surprised us had maternal adulation lowered her daughter's standard of excellence. This was never the case. From first to last Amelia set before her an ideal and strove to reach it. What she gave to the world was ever the best she could give.

Means were limited in these days, but first-rate housekeeping and rigid economy gave the home an air almost of opulence. One relaxation and one only was freely indulged in, namely, the play. Sadler's Wells and minor theatres were frequented. This love of the drama fostered in earliest years remained undiminished with Amelia to the last.

Perhaps theatre-going may be regarded in the light of a reaction. Admirable as were the moral qualities of the old Peninsular officer, his fireside influence was not inspiriting. My uncle was a taciturn man, and combined with his quiet, almost pensive habits a regularity carried to excess. He rose, read the *Times*, breakfasted, started for the bank, supped and went to bed by the clock. For society he had little taste. No wonder that his lively, high-spirited wife found some kind of stimulus necessary. The ardent play-goer was also a great reader, and her books, as well as her recreations, were shared by her little girl.

After this outburst of premature authorship, music became her absorbing occupation. It seemed, indeed, at the time, as if Amelia would make a name as pianist, composer, or even vocalist. When about fifteen she was placed under the then well-known teacher, Mrs. Mounsey Bartholomew, and for many years devoted herself entirely to pianoforte, organ, singing and harmony. I have known her practise eight hours a day, besides giving time to counterpoint. At eighteen she was a good musician, and earning money by music lessons. She also officiated as organist at a suburban church. It is curious that later in life, not only did she give up music altogether, but the very love of it seemed to desert her. Long before Egyptology was taken up, she had ceased to touch even the harmonium that stood in her study. Whenever we spent a few days in London together, we went every evening to the play; she never suggested a concert or pianoforte recital by way of variety.

Her early musical stories which appeared in *Chambers's Journal* would be acceptable to many youthful readers. Especially charming is *Alice Hoffman*, in which we trace the germ of *Barbara's History*.

In the admirable obituary notice signed J. S. C. in the *Academy* (April 23, 1892), occurs the following passage—

"From her very childhood Miss Edwards displayed talents that would have placed her in the first rank, had they been more concentrated. Her skill with the pencil was scarcely inferior to her skill with the pen; and at one time she was encouraged by competent judges to devote herself entirely to musical composition. Such versatility, whilst it contributed much to her own pleasure in life and to the fascination she exercised over others, deprived her of the rewards which she might have gained. She threw herself heart and soul into the task of the time, and then passed on with unimpaired energy to some fresh undertaking."

Nothing can be better put, and as I review these early years, the writer's conclusions are brought home to me with added force. It is just possible that, had my cousin lived a year or two longer, Egyptology would have been set aside; yet another and another subject might have taken its place, to be as eagerly pursued, as successfully mastered.

When chance brought her on a lengthened visit to Westerfield at the age of twenty-two, she appeared even to impartial eyes in the light of an Admirable Crichton. An accomplished musician and composer, a skilled draughts-woman, a clever caricaturist, a capital actress, a successful novelist, a good elocutionist, above all a connoisseur of English language and literature, what was there that she could not do? Every day brought its surprise.

It was a somewhat alarming outbreak of cholera that gave us the society of our cousin and her mother for many weeks in the old manor house already described. Perhaps Amelia never spent happier, more careless days. The warm harvest weather admitted of out-of-door life with my brothers and sisters—all, alas! like their brilliant comrade, long since sleeping in the tomb. She rode, drove, rambled, rusticated, the life and idol of the party.

One Sunday afternoon, to the intense admiration of the household and farming folk, she under-took the duties of organist at Witnesham, close by. I well remember how she varied the cut and dried programme, and how the congregation lingered spell-bound at the close of the service. She was playing us out with a voluntary of Bach's, but nobody stirred till the notes ceased. Music

THE DRIFT, WESTERFIELD, 1906

of this impassioned kind was a novelty to the naïve listeners. Hitherto the organ had seemed a mere accessory to the service.

Upon another occasion she surprised us all in a playful way. By the aid of an elder cousin, she dressed up, impersonating a young gentleman arrived from London with a letter of introduction. So successfully did she act her part, that her identity was not suspected, and only with difficulty believed in by the servants. There was no guessing what to expect from her love of pranks and, it must also be admitted, of mischief.

Elocution had been carefully studied, and in the erstwhile nursery, scene of our first meeting, she would give us delightful readings from Shakespeare and the poets. I was in the sound first sleep of early youth, when one night she came into my room and woke me up—not without difficulty, and, of course, to my considerable alarm. Laying her hand on my shoulder, she asked me in the gravest manner—

"Oh, Milly, what poet was it who said, ' Oh, sleep, thou comfortable bird'?"

The solemn query was put by no means from default of memory, but to test my own. We had been reading Keats that evening, and she wished to see how far I had been impressed.

And it was the same with personal enthusiasms; she fell in love and out of love with persons as well as with pursuits.

What was she like, this elder cousin, standing, candle in hand, mischievously waking me from midnight sleep?

A beautifully shaped, rather small head, a fine, rounded forehead, dark eyes and hair, a sensitive mouth, pallid complexion—such is the portrait I have in mind. Of medium height, she had nothing of the family spareness. I speak here of her paternal relations; even in girlhood she was of robust proportions. She was always excessively neat in dress. A stranger would at once have noted her clear enunciation and correct, somewhat amplified English.

That " pure English undefiled " was not always intelligible to our rustic neighbours, as the following anecdote will show. I was walking with her one day near our aunt's at Claydon, Suffolk, when she turned to a hobbledehoy at work close by, and asked the nearest road to Bramford Church. The lad stared agape, not understanding a syllable; I went to the rescue, and put the same query in genuine Suffolk brogue, whereupon he alertly gave the information needed.

Ah, those were happy days, days of intellectual stimulus also! Each and all were encouraged and helped in their especial pursuit by this youthful monitress. I well remember how, when I was fifteen, she sat by my side at the piano, day after day, till I performed certain of Mendelssohn's " Songs Without Words " to her liking.

On our later and never interrupted friendship I have touched elsewhere (" Reminiscences ").

I may add that Amelia Blandford Edwards was an honorary member of the Anti-Vivisection Society, and an adorer of birds. To her second surviving pet cockatoo she left an annuity by will.

She was buried in the beautiful little churchyard of Henbury, near Bristol, beside her lifelong friend, Mrs. Ellen Braysher and her daughter. On her coffin was laid a triumph of the florist's art—a hieroglyph in exquisite pansies symbolising Immortality. The memorial was placed by the companion of her lecturing tour in America, Miss Bradbury, afterwards wife of the well-known Egyptologist, Llewellyn Griffiths, who survived her friend by a few years only. As is matter of history, with the material results of her lecturing tour in America, she founded a chair of Egyptology at University College—the first in England since the days of Dorothy Wadham founded by a woman. Thus she, too, belongs to the noble band of pioneers.

IV
COVENTRY PATMORE
Poet and Mediævalist

IV

MORE justifiably perhaps than Jean Paul Richter might Coventry Patmore be styled "the only one." The German prose poet, after all, was not out of place in the eighteenth-century Fatherland. The other seemed a contemporary of Dante, Calderon, even of the Troubadours; little, indeed of the Victorian gentleman was there about him but his dress. The Franciscan garb in which he chose to be buried symbolised mediævalism of life and character. With Don Quixote, Coventry Patmore had come into the world three hundred years too late. Our epoch, as he was perpetually lamenting, possessed neither distinction, romance, nor magnanimous opportunity. Sorry medium indeed for any child of song! Yet so ruthless is the logic of facts, his best—may we not aver, his only enduring work?—belongs essentially to the modern spirit he repudiated.

For the writer who is not of his own epoch is identifiable with none. Mysticism here had dried the springs of artless fancy. A unique, a brilliant personality remained. The sweet singer in Israel was lost to the world.

About thirty-five years ago Coventry Patmore settled at Hastings. "I am now living in the very house I have longed for all my life," were almost the first words with which he greeted me.

A noble old house it is, Georgian in date, its red brick frontage beautified by a trellised magnolia, stretching on the left and raised high above the road, possessing a spacious well-wooded pleasaunce—garden hardly seems an adequately descriptive word. Few such dwellings are to be found near a large town nowadays, and the new tenant of The Mansion, as it was then called, revelled in a sense of amplitude, retirement, and dignity. Dignity, indeed, characterised the poet's household; distinction was the atmosphere that he brought with him.

It was soon after the poet's settling down that I was invited to a luncheon given in honour of the event. On entering the drawing-room my eyes immediately rested on a sumptuous woman standing in the centre of a group; she wore over her black satin dress a gold chain, not round her neck, but, doubtless with some fantastic meaning, encircling her waist. But what at once struck observers was her beaming look of triumph. Well indeed, from her own point of view, might she triumph! Had not Dr. Newman's convert been the means of bringing not only her poet, but those belonging to him, within the pale of Rome? That beaming look was always there. A cultivated woman of the world, an ardent *dévote*, she saw everything from one standpoint only. Graciousness itself, and although fond of society, this she frankly admitted. Upon one occasion, when we had discussed theological questions, fearing that she had not made her meaning transparent, she wrote to me that same evening: " You will understand me when I say that I have more fellow-feeling with an ignorant, dirty old Breton peasant woman who belongs to my religion than with any outsider, no matter how gifted." The word "timid" occurs in Mr. Gosse's three or four lines of characterisation.[1] Never did any woman possess a more imperious will than the second Mrs. Patmore; never

[1] See his delightful monograph : *Coventry Patmore.*

did any more completely wield "all the rule, one empire." Thus for many years Coventry Patmore submitted to both spiritual and domestic sway. The autocratic rule of his household during that period was strictly a feminine one.

Days of struggle, material and spiritual, were well over. Wedded to a rich, handsome and in every respect sympathetic wife, with herself, for once and for all, become an ardent Romanist, Coventry Patmore's lines were now cast in pleasant places. But prosperous circumstances left him in one respect what he had ever been. Like Shakespeare's Tiresias, he chose to be "where wit was stirring." To him, as to rare Ben Jonson, a keen wit was as dear as his nutriment. The open sesame of The Mansion was lively intellect, mental alertness, suggestiveness; rank, opulence, fashion could not turn the key. Within its walls you breathed an air of literary eclecticism and simple refinement.

The principal meal of the day—dinner, in fact —took place at twelve o'clock, the countryman's hour, light draught ale being served with unpretentious but excellent dishes. After an equally plain supper, partaken of at seven o'clock, the poet would retire, saying to his guest—seldom, indeed, was The Mansion without some congenial spirit from outside—" Now come into my study, and have a pipe and a glass of beer."

The pipe and glass might be declined, but the *tête-à-tête* was, of course, irresistible. A first-rate story-teller, full of literary reminiscence, an original and epigrammatic but wayward critic, Coventry Patmore only needed a suggestive remark or apt question, and his talk would flow in a brilliant, unbroken stream. As the blue tobacco fumes curled upwards, and the strange, lank, sardonic figure of the speaker became partly obscured, his listener would forget the man in the potency of the voice—a voice mysterious, penetrating, Dantesque, by itself, belonging not to one of ourselves, but to the olden time, an echo of the grand old days, "the days that are no more."

Here are a few jottings, mere crumbs from the rich man's table, which may give some idea of his table-talk. He had known Carlyle well, and was fond of talking about him. "Why," I asked one evening, "should Carlyle have written his *French Revolution* in the chaotic, parenthetic style of Jean Paul Richter, every sentence being a Chinese puzzle?" "Why?" he replied. "Because to put all that he had to say in clear, matter-of-fact prose would have required twenty pages instead of one. His book suited the theme; it is in itself a revolution!"

"The lack of our age is distinction," he said at another time. "What opportunity is there in these days for heroism, or in literature for really great work? Writers cannot say what they would. Some of the great books of the world are coarse. Look at Othello, Dante, Calderon—who in the present time could venture to write as freely?"

Then, sadly enough, he went on to tell me that the manuscript of a mystical poem—his best work, he considered it—had lately been burnt. "My spiritual adviser disapproved of publication," he added, with a rueful face and deep-drawn sigh.

It was in the modern novel that Coventry Patmore found mental recreation, not in stories written with a purpose, but in natural pictures of life. The super-sensuous, psychological fiction now in fashion had not as yet supplanted former ideals, and would most assuredly have been anathematised by the poet. With one or two

Coventry Patmore

startling exceptions, the lady novelists of the Victorian epoch were his favourite reading. To the Brontë sisters he was whimsically antipathetic. On the other hand, he once said to me, " I could name a hundred novels of our day each in its way as perfect as *Paradise Lost*," singling out for praise several women writers. The authoresses of *The Atélier de Lys* and of *Mr. Smith* had his suffrages.

Frank, informal hospitality charasterised the fine old house with the magnolias. One pleasant visit was made with a dear Scottish friend, the late Dr. Japp. Just twenty years ago, when staying at Hastings, the co-editor of *Good Words* expressed a wish to make Coventry Patmore's acquaintance. On asking permission to introduce my guest, came an immediate invitation to lunch, or rather early dinner. Much enlivening conversation we had at table, and much more doubtless had the two men when retiring for a *tête-à-tête* and a pipe. In a little volume of poems published for private circulation I find that Dr. Japp commemorated the day, August 12, 1888, by writing two sonnets, in one of which occurs the line—

" Sweet brotherhood, made one by sorrow's seal."

The duologue had perhaps turned upon subjects too sad and solemn for the family board.

Coventry Patmore delighted to give people little shocks. One day at table, all present being fellow-converts to Romanism but myself, he burst out with, "Nothing is a greater mistake than to think that religion makes folks happy; it makes them miserable. Look at my own case. I had planned a delightful little spree in town with X " (naming a boon companion); "we were going to see this, that and the other, and have a grand lunch together at the Criterion, when, lo! I discovered that the day fixed upon was Friday, a fast day! So I had to telegraph to X and mope at home over eggs and potatoes!"

He set as much store by genial intercourse as did Montaigne. Whilst living at the beautiful old house at Hastings which he had coveted all his life, a kind of a Harold Skimpole from America contrived to make the poet's acquaintance. "I said to myself," he told me, "'My fine fellow, you are worth fifty pounds to me; beyond that I shall not go.' He was very good company, and used to tell me most amusing stories of his own adventures in different parts of the world by the yard, not a word of any, I'll vouch for it, being true. I paid some of his bills for him, but when he asked a loan of several hundred pounds I wished him good-day.

"That fellow was one of the cleverest I ever came across," Mr. Patmore continued. "One day in the early part of our acquaintance he came to me for my advice. His wife had purchased a costume at one of the principal local drapers', but when an assistant was sent for to make certain alterations she packed it up and carried it back to the shop. What should he do? 'Go to Z——,' I said, naming my lawyer; and off he started. 'Summon the people,' said Z——, 'that is what you had better do—but wait, have you paid for the dress? If not, send a cheque and summon them afterwards.' 'On my word, I never thought of that,' exclaimed the other innocently; 'and as I don't happen to have my purse, just oblige me with your cheque for the amount!' And I'll be hanged," added Coventry Patmore, chuckling, "if he didn't bamboozle the lawyer. Instead of stepping over the way he went straight home. The dress was never paid for, and Z—— never got back his money!"

To the very last Coventry Patmore worshipped at the shrine of grace and beauty. A few years before he died he was introduced at my house to a charming young lady, and whenever we met afterwards he became dithyrambic about her. She married a little later, and I begged his autograph for a copy of his poems I had bought as a wedding gift. He thus quoted himself under a pretty inscription—

> "Nature to you was more than kind.
>   What fond perversity to dress
> So much simplicity of mind
>   In such a pomp of loveliness!"

But the compliment was felt to be overwhelming, and the volume did not appear with the other wedding gifts.

A few years later, "the waters of Shiloah that go softly" were rudely disturbed. The Mansion had changed hands, and was wanted as a residence by its new owner. All the heavier fell the blow because over against his much-loved home, Coventry Patmore had raised a handsome church in memory of his second wife, thus creating a little Catholic centre, in which he naturally occupied a foremost place. He had made many friends, too, among non-Catholics, and loved the quaint old seaboard town. Hastings also regretted the loss of the poet. Cassell's threepenny edition of *The Angel in the House* had popularised the poem among all classes. The townsfolk would turn to gaze on the tall, attenuated, erect figure in black velvet with the striking countenance as he stalked along, holding by the hand a miniature of himself, the little son born of his third marriage. There were keen regrets on both sides. The poet forfeited an ideal abode; Hastings lost distinction. But the thing had to be done, and after much painful journeying to and fro, a suitable retreat for one so fastidious was found at Lymington. The house, flanked by an old-world garden, overlooked the Solent, and was roomy, irregular, and secluded—a very fair substitute for the Georgian mansion with the magnolia. One drawback was the distance from the little church, which had to be reached by a ferry-boat. Shortly after the family installation, I was invited for a few days, and memorable days they were. Never had I found Coventry Patmore in livelier, more paradoxical mood, more thoroughly himself. As good a listener as he was a talker, he always spurred on other folk's wit; and although a bottomless gulf of antipodean opinion divided us, we were ever the best possible friends.

"You must come again in the summer," my host said at parting—we were in mid-October. "I will then take you for a long country ramble, and we will have bread and cheese and a glass of beer in an ale-house by the way."

But before the summer came he was borne to his last rest in the monastic garb symbolising not the sweet story-teller in verse, but the mystic whose most cherished work had been condemned by priestly counsel to an *auto-da-fé!*

If the gaiety of nations was not eclipsed by the death of Coventry Patmore, as I have said, the town which he had distinguished by residence keeps his memory green. Not certainly after the good French fashion. With ourselves little except military or naval history is inculcated by street nomenclature. The poet's sea-side home has as yet no street named after him, but an admirable likeness hangs in the local museum. And here a word or two may well be given to the literary, scientific and artistic progress of

Hastings within the last twenty years. Native enterprise and devotion to intellectual objects have more than atoned for the supersession or rivalship of other health resorts. The Museum, originated and indeed founded by the instrumentality of one energetic Hastingser, Mr. W. V. Crake, and housed in the Brassey Institute, gift of Lord Brassey; the Natural History Society, founded in 1893 by another Hastingser, a distinguished ornithologist, Mr. T. Parkin, F.L.S., F.Z.S., etc., now numbers four hundred members, and has done incalculable service as a stimulus to the study of science; the Egyptological Society, organised last year; the Literary Society; the Dickens Fellowship—all these form centres of intellectual activity, also of social intercourse, irrespective of circumstances, and render the premier Cinque Port something more than "a pleasant place for old ladies and gentlemen with moderate incomes to live in." Thus has the place been satirically described by a great novelist.

Nor must the great services of our curator, Mr. Ruskin Butterfield, be forgotten, to whom the Museum is immensely indebted.

V

MADAME BODICHON

The Foundress of Girton

[To face p. 89

BARBARA LEIGH SMITH BODICHON

V

MADAME BODICHON

WOMEN are deplorable ingrates towards each other. A generation of Girtonians has profited by the genius and liberality of this really great woman, their foundress, yet no literary monument has been dedicated to her memory; again and again have outsiders been compelled to vindicate it, the laurels due to her own head being placed elsewhere.

It is not, however, of the educational and social reformer that I am here going to speak, but of the conversationalist. Already at twelve years old remarkable for her apt and ready speech, as the years wore on, alike in French and English her table talk was ever full of sprightliness, pith and charm.

"How I love to hear Madame Bodichon talk!" once said a French listener to me. "Her short-comings as to accent, grammar and idiom are all forgotten, so fresh and interesting always is what she has to say."

Although married to a Frenchman and spending much time in France, B. L. S. B., as she ever signed herself, had never mastered her husband's language. Preoccupied, rather possessed by one leading idea, namely, the educational and political advance of her sex, and pursuing with equal ardour, though with less success, an artistic career, being alternately and actively interested in every great social or international movement, scant time had she for French grammar. With other leading women she had suffered at the hands of incompetent teachers, languages with other subjects having been neglected.

Here are a few of her pointed sayings—would that I could remember more!

Of novels—

Folk must die in real life : why they should die in novels, I never could see.

Of friends—

Some of our friends are roses, some are cabbages. Mrs. —— is a first-rate cabbage. To this another witty friend has added—And some are thorns!

In our Spanish travels I had excused extortion

on the part of a guide because he was a very old man. She retorted—Old age is no virtue.

On French amiability—

The reason of French good nature is that children in France are always allowed their own way, their tempers not being soured by perpetual crossing and nagging.

On a prematurely aged and beardless man—

So-and-so looks like the mummy of a boy.

On a book of travel and dealing with art galleries, written by one uninitiated in art—

The point that struck me about the book was the skill with which you have concealed your ignorance.

On the new novel of a friend—

Your story has only one fault—there is no point in it.

On superfluities—

The other day George Eliot and myself were looking at the shops in Bond Street. We both agreed that we saw nothing that we in the least wanted or desired to possess.

On men's choice of wives—

What men like in women is something that smiles. Many prefer little rags of women.

On her sex's lot—

Childbearing is the battlefield of women.

On a sentimental lady saying, after revisiting the scenes of her early youth, that she felt as if by a longer stay she should recover her " childish innocence "—

I hope you have not lost it, have you?

On Victor Hugo's dramas—

To my thinking they are as fine as Shakespeare's.

On Zola and his school—

Such stories are the reverse of realism. They are non-realistic because they do not represent life as it is.

On marriage—

Nothing delights me more than to hear of any man being refused by a woman. Such experiences put men in their right place.

On George Eliot—

I suppose the time will come when all educated folks will write like George Eliot.

Madame Bodichon

Presumably her meaning was that slipshod futility would give way to well-thought-out utterance and expression, also to strictly philosophic studies of life and human nature.

To a friend presenting a somewhat idealised photograph of herself—a quite anti-Aristotelian view, by the way, and suggestive of Cromwell—

Take this back and give me one with all your lines in it.

To the students of her College of Girton—

You must make laws for yourselves.

About herself and her unorthodoxy, alike voluntary and involuntary—

I am a rich woman, and therefore when I die there will be no fuss about burying an unbaptized person in consecrated ground.

On setting up in her own house a night school, the teacher being a Wesleyan and the teaching non-sectarian—

I need not fear clerical interference, because I am rich.

To a Frenchwoman, wife of an officer garrisoned in a remote Algerian station—

Take my advice and regularly devote one hour a day to the reading of a good book. You will find therein a sovereign remedy for ennui and the feeling of emptiness you complain of.

On a Christmas present—

I sent the X—— family a turkey. It was the only kind of present they would understand and appreciate.

On Darwin's *Earth Worms*—

What a wonderful book! Who after perusal can help believing in Evolution, and that everything improves as we go on?

On misapplied, especially wasted, faculties and talents—

A penknife should never be used for the purpose of cutting a rope.

This remark of my friend recalls a passage in Selden's *Table Talk:* "Little things will do great works when the great things will not. If I should take a pin from the ground, a little pair of tongs will do it when a great pair will not."

On the vague description of a flowery Algerian plain in a friend's book—

"Fair and fragrant children of the waste."—

Bosh! Why not have taken the trouble to name a flower or two?

Here she recalls a maxim of Horace as to the value of particularisation. Bosh, it may be mentioned, was a favourite expletive with her, serving the purpose of Mr. Burchell's "Fudge!"

On table talk to a friend—

Your own gift that way is that you ask most interesting questions.

On a bit of wretchedly cramped handwriting—

No one with any greatness of soul would write such a hand as that.

On a group of highly esteemed people—

First-rate folks, but dull as ditchwater.

This remark recalls Kinglake's witty verdict on a great statesman: "A good man of the worst description," and Milton's line on Satan's fit of self-reproach—"Stupidly good."

On converts to Romanism—

When any friends of mine go over to Rome a gulf yawns between us. In a sense they are wholly lost to me.

On high thought and small snobberies—

I lunched the other day at the Deanery (with Dean and Lady Augusta Stanley) to meet Mr. Gladstone. There was served a cut gooseberry pie. That pie doing double duty is a standing lesson to my housekeeper, and now she has to bring to table pies that have been begun.

On other snobberies—

My leg-of-mutton dinners, as I call them, I began in Algeria. Whenever rich people dined with me I gave them just anything. When poorly paid French functionaries were invited I always provided a sumptuous repast.

In London the leg-of-mutton dinners were also the rule, and not, perhaps, always accepted with a good grace. When the table was set the hostess would also go round with a bottle of water and well dilute the half-filled decanters of sherry and claret.

Mme. Bodichon had a rough-and-ready way of treating practical details. When travelling with her in Spain she found me puzzling over pesetas and doubloons and the rest—

"Why trouble your head about Spanish

money?" she said, and bringing out her purse laid on the table an English shilling, a two-shilling piece, a half-sovereign, and a sovereign. "Now," she added, poising each coin and its Spanish equivalent by turns on her finger, "the weight of gold and silver will tell you nearly enough what the money represents." A neat and expeditious way of doing international sums, it seemed to me.

Other travelling maxims were equally original.

Always travel with plenty of luggage. You are then sure to meet with attention and get the best of everything.

Another maxim appropriate now-a-days to France as well as to the Spain of forty years ago was this—

Stand on the platform by your handbags and look helpless.

In many a provincial station to this day no porters appear: the traveller on arriving has to address himself to the station-master for help.

An advanced Liberal, a warm advocate of social reform, a practical-minded thinker, this noble Englishwoman was not always keen-sighted either in political matters or in judging character.

"Thank Heaven," she said exuberantly, when John Bright's motion according votes to the agricultural labourer was passed—"we shall see no more Tory *régimes* in England."

The Act was followed by twenty years of Conservative Government!

Misreading of character, or rather enthusiasm carried to the point of infatuation, would lead to disillusion. Upon one occasion she was thus nonplussed.

After a prolonged eulogy of some new *protégée* whose numberless gifts and charms were to raise her to social and intellectual eminence—who was, indeed, to set the world on fire in many places, an interlocutor asked mildly—

"What has this paragon, this feminine Admirable Crichton achieved thus to raise your expectations?"

She thought for a moment or two, and at last got out—

"Well, she has given birth to a beautiful baby."

"My dear friend," retorted the other, "she will

not attain immortality by becoming the mother of a baby, however beautiful."

Like Herbert Spencer, whom she knew well, she loved to propound questions.

Thus, especially to younger friends, she would put the ethical problem—

Would you rather possess beauty, or be the cause of beauty in others?

She said that with herself the latter choice would kick the beam, meaning that the gift of physical attractions and charm, of æsthetic gifts, opportunities and surroundings, would be out-weighed by the power of putting all these in some measure within reach of others not thus endowed.

We can generally appraise folks, *i. e.* thinking folks, by their maxims. A favourite citation with her was from the Koran—"If you have only enough money in your purse wherewith to buy flowers or bread, choose flowers and let the bread go."

Yet, intense as was her love of beauty, she ever remained practical of the practical. With B. L. S. B., in the words of the great Locke, knowledge was seeing. With a few wild flowers in her hand she would make children or the uninitiated understand points of vegetable physiology not easily got at through books.

And as there are limitations even in the highest developments of intellect and character, so was it here. Herbert Spencer somewhere says that the proposition, two parallel lines can never meet, is unverifiable, because two parallel lines can never be followed infinitely. With Mme. Bodichon, knowledge was seeing, as far as it went, but there ever remained the beyond, the unverifiable.

Had her brother, Benjamin Leigh Smith, as she fondly hoped, discovered the North Pole in 1870-1, her first query on his return would have been—

"Well, Ben, and what lies beyond?"

Like the immortal Vathek of "England's richest son," she "wished to know everything; even sciences that did not exist."

On the *Grand Peut-être* of Rabelais, the questions that have occupied philosophers and mystics since Plato's *Phædo*, she remained silent, so beset was she, not by a sense of her rights, but of her duties, that, like Wilberforce, she "had no time to think about her soul." Confident in the causes for which she had sacrificed so much, rationalist in the highest sense of the word, ardently believing that humanity was on the upward path, she accepted the inevitable with unswerving courage and calm. Neither disillusion, broken health, pain nor grief had power to shake that commanding spirit. In a certain vital sense she was as unpractical as the most flighty-headed. A woman of ardent faith in individuals and causes and of abnormal activities, Goethe's excellent maxim for intellectual workers, "un-hasting, unresting," she could never take to heart, always trying to make twelve hours do the duty of twenty-four, always taxing her mental and physical powers to the straining point.

I used to say to her, "My dear friend, excellently as you husband your material resources, in another and equally important sense you are ever on the brink of insolvency, without a pennyworth of reserve force to your credit."

And, true enough, bankruptcy came upon her as a thief in the night.

It was during the winter of 1866–7 that, amid Algerian surroundings, I first knew this splendid, inspiring personality. Then in her prime, words, looks, gestures betokened "the wild joys of living," soul, mind, heart full to overflowing with warmest sympathies and lofty ideals.

Ten years later she was suddenly stricken down, becoming a wreck, a mere shadow of her former self; from that time unto the end, which did not come till fifteen years later, she remained a confirmed invalid, entirely cut off from former activities and "the cheerful ways of men."

One of her last acts was to send a cheque to the Women's Franchise Society, and by her will, subject to certain annuities, the larger portion of her fortune accrued to Girton College.

Turning to the pages of that first-rate compendium of knowledge, Chambers's *Encyclopædia*, 1892, under the head of Girton College and Women's Rights (the articles being written by a woman), I vainly look for even the name of Barbara Bodichon. Certes, it is not the gratitude of women towards each other that will set any poet mourning!

A word or two concerning the personality of this educational and social pioneer, steadfast upholder of noble causes, born internationalist and gifted water-colourist.

For, as was the case with Amelia Blandford

Edwards, she strove after eminence in too many fields. Had, for instance, all her energies been devoted to painting, she would very likely have attained the recognition and status passionately longed for but never attained. Her charming, hastily dashed-off impressions lacked learning and solidity. She paid the price of a many-faceted mentality.

"Barbara Bodichon's portrait is in every European picture gallery" was wont to say a much-travelled friend of her childhood. Titianesque, indeed, were her superb colouring, golden hair, blue eyes, perfectly shaped mouth, and proportions humanly, not classically, beautiful. There was no cold, stately classicism about features or figure, life exuberant and exuberating to the very full emanated from her presence, an afflatus once calling forth Browning's ejaculation—

"Madame Bodichon, what a benediction to see you!"

And a benediction to how many was her friendship!

VI

WILLIAM ALLINGHAM

Poet and Causeur

VI

WILLIAM ALLINGHAM

A POET of unfulfilled promise, a delightful talker, an ungrudgeful but too assiduous cultivator of bigger men than himself, was this close friend.

As the shadow of a spreading oak keeps light and air from slenderer growths below, so the near neighbourhood and potent influence of giant genius may prove fatal to those less gifted. Had the young Irish poet, of English, not Celtic, origin, remained on the banks of his beloved Ballyshannon instead of becoming a Londoner and fairly prosperous man of letters, comrade of Rossetti and his set, a worshipper of George Eliot, Tennyson, and above all, Carlyle, he might have attained the position he longed for but missed.

"I thank you for still regarding me as a poet," he wrote to me, a few years before his death, and upon another occasion in writing he deplored his apparent indolence, due to lack of aspiration.

He began well. *Laurence Bloomfield* in Ireland all but attained the fortune of another book god-fathered by Gladstone. Who now-a-days reads or even has ever heard of that pretty narrative poem in five thousand decasyllabic lines? Its appearance did indeed attract that great statesman, and brought the poet a Civil List pension, which he enjoyed all his life, and a post in the Excise.

The first flush of success, the fair, if not brilliant aurora, had grown dim when I used to walk and talk with William Allingham for five hours at a stretch. Our acquaintance began in the Isle of Wight in 1868—I believe, or thereabouts—his location as a Custom House Commissioner then being at Yarmouth. By this time he had already passed Dante's climacteric and was within a few years of fifty. Already, too, he was full of whimsies which his hosts had to put up with, often to their great inconvenience. From the date of his removal to London soon after our first meeting until his marriage in 1874 he was many times my fellow-guest of Madame Bodichon at Roberts-

SCALANDS GATE, 1867

[To face p. 109

bridge. Long rambles during the day with a companion were not enough for him. As soon as the household was asleep, privileged with a house key, he would sally forth, as Dr. Bodichon used to say—*pour chercher des inspirations*, a seeker, most often in vain, after poetic vision. It would not unusually be long after midnight when he would return, noisily making his way to the pantry and there helping himself to anything that took his fancy.

A little time before noon, sometimes indeed between ten and eleven o'clock, he would quit his bedroom, of course a special breakfast having to be prepared for him. Upon one occasion he returned from a late afternoon expedition in the rain with—as he feared—damp socks. Before the kitchen fire a goose was spitted for the seven o'clock dinner.

Coolly removing the old-fashioned roaster with outstretched, unbooted feet, he seated himself till perfectly reassured on the matter of damp foot gear. So delightful was his company that hostess and French host let him go his own way unrebuked.

He dearly loved a thunderstorm. I well

remember setting out with him for the railway station, a mile and a quarter off, when a terrific thunderstorm, with a persistent downpour, came on.

Complacently he trudged along, chatting of books and things, the most enticing weather could not have improved his spirits or his conversation. With a much surprised look, he asked, as I started at a blinding flash—

" Do you mind this? "

The thought of taking shelter at one of the cottages passed on the way never occurred to him, and we continued our walk.

As a young man he visited Weimar, and thus he was characterised by an Englishman who had been his friend and cicerone in the little Thuringian Athens. " I seemed to revive my own youth in William Allingham's personality," said the Grand Duchess's English secretary, Mr. Marshall, to me in 1871.

" He is no echo," was George Eliot's appraisement.

Without being a wit or brilliant talker, he had happy turns, and as a critic his generosity knew no bounds.

"One peach is better than two" was a saying of his that his friend, Madame Bodichon, loved to quote.

On poets and literature he would discourse airily all day long. To quote a Spenserian coinage, I might call his talk airified, on each topic coming the breeze of personality, something fresh, invigorating, and belonging to himself.

Later in life his views on many vital questions underwent topsy-turvydom. "We now shake hands over a bottomless gulf of opposite opinion," I wrote to him, when the Benedict, become a happy husband and proud father, was enjoying the full sunshine of prosperity at Witley near Haslemere.

He was now a strong Conservative, anti-Home Ruler and anti-progressist even in matters intellectual. "Our girls are now learning Latin," he sighed, when alluding to some licentious classic, and elsewhere he lamented that Lord Byron "had neglected his duties as a peer of the realm."

In his lately published Diaries he wrote of his old friend M. B.-E. as "a Republican" (not qualifying the epithet with "as far as France is concerned") "and a Home Ruler." *Tête-à-tête*

talk with us two in those later interviews recalled
the famous dictum of La Fontaine—

> "La dispute est d'un bon secours
> Sans elle, on dormirait encore."

We rarely agreed and never got heated in
discussion.

But with Liberalism and a certain ever-increas-
ing faddiness had not vanished the old charm
and affectionateness.

Dear William Allingham! He never made a
fourth with Browning, Swinburne and Tennyson,
but could he revisit the scene of early hopes and
ambitions, would doubtless feel satisfied. Several
of his smaller poems for once and for all are
incorporated into English literature, are now
indeed on the way to their centenary—in Dr.
Johnson's opinion, the earnest and seal of
imperishable fame.

It is now sixty years since his *Day and Night
Songs* first appeared. A memorial edition of
favourite pieces is yet to come, meanwhile few
anthologies are without a posy from the Allingham garden. Here are lines worthily commemorated by a fastidious and witty critic (Birrell's
In the Name of the Bodleian)—

William Allingham

"Four ducks on a pond,
A grass bank beyond;
A blue sky of spring,
White clouds on the wing,
How little a thing
To remember for years—
To remember with tears!"

One of my own especial favourites is "Wayside Flowers."

"Pluck not the wayside flower,
It is the traveller's dower:
A thousand passers-by
Its beauties may espy,
May win a touch of blessing
From Nature's mild caressing.
The sad of heart perceives
A violet under leaves,
Like some fresh budding hope;
The primrose on the slope
Like spots of sunshine dwells,
And cheerful message tells
Of kind, renewing power;
The nodding bluebell's dye
Is drawn from happy sky.
Then spare the wayside flower,
It is the traveller's dower!"

VII

AN AFTERNOON WITH LORD JOHN RUSSELL

VII

IT was in the summer of 1868 that I had the honour of meeting the "Lycurgus of the Lower House," as Sydney Smith called the great little man of the famous *Punch* cartoons.

A few months after making my home in Kensington, I received a note from Sir Edwin Chadwick to this effect—Might he drive me on a certain afternoon to an industrial school—I forget the name—where Lord and Lady Russell would join us. The object of the visit was to show the Prime Minister over the institution.

Of Sir Edwin Chadwick a word or two may be necessary. No man was ever more useful in his especial field, and perhaps no man has been more completely forgotten.

The great authority on sanitation—rather I should call him the inventor of the science—was an old friend of Madame Bodichon, and at her house in Sussex I had just before made his acquaintance. Like all, or most, enthusiasts, he was an interminable talker on his own subject, and during our two or three days' co-guestship I had become pretty well indoctrinated with some of his theories.

Never was a more thorough-going reformer. He was the Mohammed of drain-pipes, the Columbus of conduits, alike the prophet and apostle of concrete. The late learned but little known Hellenist, Mr. Watkiss Lloyd, used to say that if ever Sir Edwin lost his mental balance he would imagine himself to be a universal drain-pipe, the conduit of the universe. But that solid head of his could take in more ideas than one, and as secretary to the Poor Law Board for five-and-twenty years he had worked hard in the causes of children's labour, education, and preventive disease. At the time I mention he was an indefatigable member of the Social Science Association and of the Statistical Society. Numbers for this extraordinary man possessed an overweening fascination. In listening to him one almost became convinced that the salvation of society lay in statistics. Hence his invitation to Lord John Russell. The great statesman was to see for himself the enormous gain of large agglomerations. Those schools of forty years ago were, I believe, looked upon in the light of models.

Punctual to their appointment, Lord and Lady Russell arrived—the latter a quiet, amiable-looking lady, of whom I remember nothing more, the former as striking a contrast to his host as could well be conceived.

Sir Edwin Chadwick, although three years younger than Lord Russell, looked his senior. Big, heavy, with florid cheeks and flowing hair and beard, Sir Edwin moved slowly and deliberately, all physical force being focused in the vocal organs.

Why attempt any portraiture of the "little great man," familiar to us all in those wonderful cartoons? Do we not all know what that statesman was like who, as was the case with another intellectual giant, Sir Isaac Newton, came into the world so tiny that he could hardly have filled a quart pot?

Bodily divergences of the pair were not less striking than the contrast of port and behaviour. From the moment of entering the building to departure our cicerone's tongue continued active.

Through every part we were conducted under a running fire of volubly uttered facts and figures. His visitor was to go away enlightened as to every particular of installation, management, and, above all, of cost. The arithmetical totals, sum-totals, and averages now poured into Lord Russell's patient ear must have recalled Budget night. A patient ear, did I say? If the listener only from time to time put in a brief query, it was simply because he had no opportunity of doing more.

Whether he sympathised with his interlocutor's views it was impossible to say. As Sir Edwin Chadwick dilated on the subject at that time uppermost in his mind—namely, the economy of the system here illustrated, the immense saving of such schools on an enormous scale—the other remained passive.

But it was when we reached the dormitories that half-a-dozen words revealed the man, the "all-saving common sense" and practical wisdom characterising the great politician.

With more than his usual exuberance, Sir Edwin now pointed to the scores upon scores of snowy beds in one enormous sleeping-room, its lofty proportions, its numerous windows reaching from ceiling to floor, and facing due south.

Those large windows facing south arrested Lord Russell's attention. Turning to his host, he asked quietly—

"What about the children's eyes?"

Unprovided with shutters, curtains, or anything in the shape of a blind, this dormitory would be flooded with light during many months, half of the night being thus turned into dazzling day. Lord Russell's quick, unerring, and ever ready intelligence evidently called up a picture of tired youngsters tossing restlessly on their pillows, of weak eyes injured perhaps for life, of ophthalmic cases here engendered. And all for want of a little of what Sterne calls "household good sense!"

Lady Russell, if I remember rightly, had also something to say on the subject, but whether or no Sir Edwin was struck by his visitor's criticism and whether any practical result came of it, I do not know. The incident remained in my memory, illustrating as it forcibly did, not only the multifarious channels into which a great intellect will flow, but the limitations so often found in genius. In his own field the apostle of the drain-pipe might fairly be so styled. Yet a merest common-place connected with his own special subject had thus escaped him, and was left to the statesman to find out. What more important in orphanages than the care of children's eyes?

I never saw Lord John Russell after the courteous leave-taking that summer afternoon; but many years later I took tea and dined with Sir Edwin Chadwick and his wife and daughter at Richmond. So far back as 1854 his great services as a social and administrative worker had been rewarded by a Government pension. He was now enjoying to the full Macbeth's ideal of old age, good repute, affectionate intercourse, easy circumstances, and the consciousness of having nobly served his country in pacific walks.

The summer afternoon was superb, and till the dinner-bell rang, hosts and guests remained in the pretty suburban garden. It was a pleasant picture to carry away in one's memory, the veteran reformer chatting quietly with this friend and that, amid his roses, the fire of propagandism burnt out, instead his eyes beaming with the tempered radiance of well-earned repose.

He was no longer the untiring pioneer of sanitation and hygiene—for had I not heard him discuss the virtues of concrete with Madame Bodichon throughout a long summer day?

Cheap, good, solid workmen's dwellings at that time had engrossed his attention. Lighter topics now held the field.

After an interval of more than half-a-century comes to light a noble testimony from another and equally noble pioneer. As these pages are prepared for press I come upon the following testimony to his lifelong friend from John Stuart Mill (*Correspondence*, 1910).

Writing to a Scotch correspondent in 1868, concerning Sir Edwin's fitness for Parliament, Mill thus closes a very long list of his friend's achievements in public fields : " I have touched only on main points, for to go through all the minor but important matters of public interest which he has helped forward would take up far too much time and space. I may say in brief that he is one of the contriving and organising minds of the age; a class of mind of which there are very few, and still fever who apply those qualities to the practical business of government. He is, however, one of the few men I have known who have a passion for the public good; and nearly the whole of his time is devoted to it in one form or another."

It is something to have known men like Sir Edwin Chadwick, something is it also to have so much as listened to men like Mill. I suppose there are not many now who, like myself, heard the great apostle of Liberty speak at St. James's Hall in the 'sixties. Stereotyped on my memory is that stupendous personality. In the look of unshakable conviction—so admirably rendered in both portraits accompanying the *Correspondence* —of a thinker whose mind upon the weightiest subjects was irrevocably made up, from whose ethical verdicts was no appeal, his countenance had something sublime, even awful of rigidity and adamant implacableness. I felt as I gazed that chance, destiny, inclination and weakness could exercise no kind of sway over this man, that here were the iron will, the unflinching self-oblivion of which the Luthers, Savonarolas, and Sir John Eliots are made.

Of the ever-regretted misses in life, this souvenir recalls one.

Mill and Spencer it has been my privilege to

see, if not to know; that other one who "had the name among the three mighties" of thought and wisdom I once missed by just five minutes.

"Just five minutes sooner and you would have found Carlyle here," exclaimed William Allingham one afternoon when I called upon him and his wife, then living in Trafalgar Square, Chelsea.

This by the way. In Lord Fitzmaurice's valuable *Life of Lord Granville*, which work is indeed a Parliamentary history of England from 1815 to 1891, occurs the following citation. Under date November 24, 1867, the late Lord Coleridge wrote to a friend—

"I had a very pleasant dinner with Lord John on Wednesday. We were but seven—Lowe, Bruce, Lord Granville, Baines, Jowett, Lord Russell himself, and I. He sat me beside him, and was most courteous and a great deal more kindly and genial than I expected to find him. After dinner he made us a little speech about education, which he (rightly, I think) considers *the* question of the day, and explaining and recommending some resolutions of his which he purposes to move in the House of Lords. I was more struck with his simplicity and a certain nobleness of thought about him than with his cleverness. His ideas were commonplace enough, but when Lord Granville said that 'he feared that forcing some point on might break up the party,' Lord Russell said quite simply that nothing would ever be done if people were afraid of such consequences, and that a great party could not fail more nobly than in trying for the attainment of such an object; but I saw quite enough to be sure that he was very self-*willed*, which is perhaps almost as bad."

In an earlier page of these deeply interesting volumes, Lord Granville speaks of "Johnny's great speech on Education," which, he adds, did not, he feared, advance matters much. This was in 1856.

Like many another statesman, this one had literary ambitions. He was a voluminous writer, and among the long list of his works are a novel and two tragedies now forgotten. Some second-rate verses are inserted in Sir Spencer Walpole's excellent biography.

In *Gryll Grange*, 1859, the last but not least diverting of Peacock's subacid novels, Lord John Russell is travestied under the title of Lord

Michin Malicho,[1] Lord Brougham being coupled with him as Lord Facing-both-ways. The pair are called "arch-quacks who have taken to merry-andrewsing in a new arena, which they call the science of Pragmatics" (Social Science).

In another passage we read—"Mr. Mac Borrowdale in his lecture touched upon Reform. The stone which Lord Michin Malicho— who was the Gracchus of the last Reform and is the Sisyphus of this—has been so laboriously pushing uphill, is for the present deposited at the bottom of the Limbo of Vanity."

Milton's line—"Of whom to be dispraised were no small praise"—is often appropriate to the cynical author just cited.

The great little Johnny might be a poetaster and a dreamer, all the same I am proud to have known that great politician and unswerving advocate of Reform.

[1] Hamlet, "Marry, this is *miching malecho;* it means mischief."

VIII
TEA WITH CHRISTINA ROSSETTI

TEA WITH CHRISTINA ROSSETTI

VIII

TEA WITH CHRISTINA ROSSETTI

IN a pretty little bucolic Christina Rossetti describes the feeding of motherless lambs in northern England from teapots. So spontaneous and touching are the verses that we feel they must be the outcome of experience, a little improvisation called forth by an unwonted sight. What, then, was my surprise when I met the poet and discovered that she was urban of the urban, not only town-bred but townish, the last person in the world from whom one could expect a pastoral?

Our meeting-place, and every circumstance connected with it, were worthy of her muse.

The season was midsummer, and the weather was both pictorial and poetical, such as painters try to portray and poets put into verse.

Tea was spread on a little lawn bordered with carelessly-kept, old-fashioned flowers—sweet-williams, columbines, larkspurs, York and Lancaster roses—hardly a flower familiar to us all from childhood but was here growing in profusion. Beyond this beautiful but homely pleasance were

> "Places of nestling green for poets made."

Little footways—paths there were none—led into coppice woods, wild strawberries, now ripe, gleaming ruby red among the moss, hazel-trees showing rich clusters, honeysuckle and wild rose scenting the air. Above this brilliant foliage the colour deepened, sombre green merging into purple shadow. We were indeed hemmed round by

> "The blessed woods of Sussex, I can hear them still
> around me,
> With their leafy tide of greenery still rippling up the
> wind."

In the rear stood a rose-embowered cottage, its chimney-corner showing a goodly roll-call. On the walls poets, painters, philosophers, and political economists had left their sign-manual. Here, with their noble-minded hostess, Madame Bodichon, George Eliot and George Henry Lewes had held high discourse. Here the great French painter Daubigny had dashed in his autograph, accompanying it with a tiny landscape. Here Dante Rossetti, William Morris, and William Allingham had discussed poetry and art.

Here the blind Professor Fawcett had discussed with his hostess political economy. And here was matured the scheme of the first women's university opened in England—namely, Girton College.

Our little party numbered four. These were the hostess, who was then, as William Rossetti has recently described her, in the plenitude of mental and physical powers, her abundant golden hair a glory to behold, with a nobility of face much more striking than mere beauty, Mrs. Rossetti, the poetess, and myself.

Of her mother I remember nothing. Christina was at this time about forty, a plainly-dressed, gaunt, rather jerky woman, shy in manner, and very reticent. Such at least was my impression. Herself an inspiring talker, our hostess could always set shy folks at their ease. On this occasion she naturally chatted of suggestive topics—gardening, flowers (she was a very good botanist in the practical sense), the beauty of her environment, and so on. Madame Bodichon was also a very clever artist, and she next spoke of a beautiful sunrise she had lately seen.

Then the poetess by her side broke silence.

"I have never seen the sun rise in my life," she observed quietly.

The confession came to me as quite a little shock. That a poetess should reach middle life without having once beheld Nature's great pageant seemed unbelievable, of one, moreover, who had written how

"By fits and starts looks down the waking sun."

On second thoughts the matter was easy of explanation. Town born and town bred, an invalid and untravelled, her opportunities of seeing the sun rise had perhaps been few. Her genius, moreover, was rather subjective than given to outward impression; inner life, especially devotional life, appealing to her more than the world around. Yet in some of her happiest moods she could write charmingly of Nature, as in "The Lambs of Grasmere" (1860). I cite two verses—

"The upland flocks grew starved and thinned;
   Their shepherds scarce could feed the lambs,
Whose milkless mothers butted them,
   Or who were orphaned of their dams.
The lambs, athirst for mothers' milk,
   Filled all the place with piteous sounds;
Their mothers' bones made white for miles
   The pastureless, wet pasture-ground.

"Day after day, night after night,
   From lamb to lamb the shepherds went
With teapots for the bleating mouths
   Instead of Nature's nourishment.
The little shivering, gaping things
   Soon knew the step that brought them aid,
And fondled the protecting hand,
   And rubbed it with a woolly head."

That little poem, simple as it is, has a winningness of its own. How one wishes that the writer had lived more in the country, and given us more like it! And how one regrets the circumstances leading surely to one of the strangest admissions ever uttered by a poet: "I have never seen the sun rise in my life!"

IX
H. B. BRABAZON (BRABBY)

IX

ABOUT thirty years ago my old friend, Mr. H. Brabazon Brabazon—"Brabby" to his circle —was showing me some recent sketches in the salon of the Hôtel du Jura, Dijon. At that time, although considerably past his prime, "Brabby" as an artist was absolutely unknown. A few, a very few friends, indeed, knew and appreciated his subtle gifts as a colourist, but the most enthusiastic of these never for a single moment dreamed that he would ever make a name, much less money by the brilliant splashes dashed off so rapidly. It was not till a decade and a half later that the then septuagenarian, like Byron, woke to find himself famous!

Upon the occasion in question, the sketches, the striking personality of the artist, and my own unsophisticated admiration attracted an elderly fellow-countryman, apparently a business man taking his holiday. Noticing his hardly-restrained

139

interest, Mr. Brabazon kindly invited him to join us, for his benefit beginning the show over again.

That ordinary-looking stranger proved not only to be a fine art-critic, but, as afterwards turned out, to possess the gift of prophecy.

His delight in the lovely suggestions of Italian skies and sunsets—Mr. Brabazon was returning from the South—knew no bounds; perhaps, indeed, savoured of intemperance.

"A second Turner, a Turner!" he reiterated with the fervour of Gratiano's—"a second Daniel, a Daniel."

Even later, and after attaining recognition, no one would have more keenly reluated at the comparison than the artist himself. At the time it was spoken the eulogium merely evoked a smile, and in after years he never alluded to the incident. It was a case of "ships that pass in the night." That chance-met conjurer of Fortune's most cherished gift to genius, namely, deserved fame, with a "Thank you, from my heart, sir," and a warm handshake, passed out of his ken, and, as it seemed, memory.

But up to a certain point the vaticination became fact. Happy throughout every circumstance of his life, Mr. Brabazon was most fortunate in this : he appeared precisely when wanted, neither a day too soon nor a day too late. For it is with genius—of which he certainly possessed a touch—as with flowers and fruit, the ill-timed chestnut blossoms, flavourless strawberries at Yuletide. The *à propos* here, as in every phase of human endeavour, forms a turning-point, a keynote of success, using the word in its best sense. Impressionism was in the air. As a kindred spirit he was immediately received into the brotherhood.

To return, however, to those days of pure delight in his art, of perpetual revelling in natural beauty. I well remember how, after that half-hour just described, he set out, sketch-book in hand, halting to dash in an impression whenever the humour seized him. Unlike Mr. Hamerton and Mr. Augustus Hare, he never during his travels enjoyed the distinction of an arrest. Could, indeed, a spy-scared outside Bedlam have discovered in dear Brabby's lovely vaguenesses the faintest similitude to fortress or strategic defences? It might, indeed, be said of some of his sketches that you may find anything you like therein, just as all kinds of scenes may be pictured in hot cinders. To detectives Mr. Brabazon and his sketch-book would appear mere English eccentricity. Anyhow, whilst the equally harmless authors of *Round my House* and of so many useful guide-books were taken before the French police on a charge of espionage, the afterwards famous impressionist got off scot-free. A spoilt child of fairy godmothers, being born to a handsome estate, he was spoiled wherever he went. In Rome and other Italian towns he loved to be locked inside churches whilst the sacristans retired for dinner, and these ever humoured him, doubtless imagining that they had to do with a pietist, or perhaps lunatic, who, nevertheless, had sense enough to reward them for their pains!

What a perpetual ecstasy were his entire eighty and odd years! Very little of the time was spent in his beautiful Sussex home, auspiciously having a brother-in-law to take the burdens of property off his shoulders, being absolutely free, able to give every moment of his time to Southern sunshine, art, music, and the society of kindred spirits. Now he would be in Spain, financing some musical *protégé*, now in Rome on the same errand, now at Amiens with Ruskin, studying that wondrous cathedral—a world of art in itself—now at Weimar enjoying music with Liszt, everywhere following the sun, everywhere absorbing and dispensing happy influences.

A real artist in his way, an accomplished musician, Mr. Brabazon's personality was more fascinating than his gifts. There is a pathetic, a word of measureless psychological import used by Swift. He speaks somewhere in those unique outpourings to Stella of a *charmless* personage. What a terrible immortality! When that is said, all else is said, whether the question be of human beings or their achievements. Goethe has poetised the same thought,

"Was nicht reizt ist todt"—

What does not charm (in art or literature) is dead. Never for a moment of his existence charmless himself, Mr. Brabazon for the most part most skilfully contrived to avoid the charmless alike personal, cosmographic and social. County benches, local boards, politics, the routine obligations and amusements of a country gentleman he delegated to others. His mission in life was to imbibe and dispense ideal beauty, to enforce, in so far as in him lay, the great Aristotelean dictum that art consists in capture of the beautiful.

Some human lives are a drama, others are an unsolved chord, others—alas! the majority—a mere accompaniment to the tune of "Go and get your hair cut," or the latest music-hall ditty. Brabby's was a lyric, simple, rounded off, mellifluous as that perfect little song in a forgotten drama—

"A sunny shaft did I behold,
  From sky to earth it slanted,
And poised therein, a bird so bold,
  Sweet bird, thou wert enchanted!"

Pensive, even grief - stricken moments, of course, were his as every one's; tragic experiences, I should say, he missed altogether. Artistic disillusions and the pathetic in art would ever bring tears to his eyes. Perhaps one of his greatest mortifications was the fact of never having heard Liszt play! Cordial and prolonged as was the intercourse of the two, the great virtuoso, as a virtuoso at the time, had become an aged, worn-out man, and on no account could any one, even his most intimate friends, beg him to touch the piano. Mr. Brabazon's eyes would fill whenever I alluded to my own privileges a decade and a half before. I had often heard Liszt's indescribable playing when at Weimar in 1871. My old friend loved to hear of the magician, although the relation would bring poignant regret.

Another matter for grieving to which he would refer years after was a missed summer in Algeria. It happened, I think in 1869, that his great friend, Madame Bodichon, then living at Mustapha Supérieur, had lent her handsome villa conjointly to Mrs. Bridell Fox, herself no mean artist, and to an old Anglo-Frenchman, a follower of Fourier, and his wife. Mr. Brabazon was included in the invitation, but for some reason or other did not accept it.

"What a mistake I made, I have never forgiven myself!" he used to say. "What sunsets, what effects, what impressions I should have obtained. And then the society! That dear old M. Hawke and his wife ever harping on the golden age before us, and not behind; no, never again shall I have such an opportunity."

"The golden age is before and not behind us," was the watchword of the Fouriérist community.

The various organisations founded by Fourier and his followers came to naught. In Hawthorne's romance, *The Blithedale Romance*, their dreams will long live. And in every forward social movement we discern the ideas of men regarded by their contemporaries as crazed fanatics.

With the regeneration of the world, economic, civic and political, Mr. Brabazon had nothing to do. His energies concerned things intangible, transcendental, of having a mission he never certainly dreamed. All the same, to this most modest nature, to one who always spoke of doing this or that "in my little way," with what joy came praise and renown! With what surprise, too, came the seal of both, the final, the indispensable, the delightful attestation of value! Not only were his sketches now laudated, exhibited, in everybody's mouth, they fetched money, the least interpretative scenes had their price.

The last fifteen years of his long life—he was far on the way to ninety when he peacefully passed away—formed a triumphal progress. A Brabazon Exhibition was now an annual artistic event. Before he died, selections of his work had been purchased for the British Museum and the

Picture Gallery of New York, whilst scores, hundreds of lovely things had found their way to provincial and private galleries.

Favoured of fortune throughout life, Brabby has been felicitous in his apotheosis. The simplest, most appropriate and most touching monument possible recalls his memory. The idea and execution were both the work of a lady, his beloved niece, and it is much to be hoped that similar memorials may relieve the monotony and commonplaceness of our villages.

Within bowshot of his home and on his own property stands a tithe barn, one of the few now remaining throughout the country. Restored and embellished within and without, this relic of feudality has been transformed into an art gallery, and under the name of " The Brabazon Museum " was opened with much enthusiasm nearly a year ago.

Around its walls are choicest Brabazons, Italian, Spanish and French views, Sussex landscape and many exquisite flower-pieces. A loan collection of local antiquities has been added by the committee of the Hastings Museum. The charge of admission is 3*d*., and tea can be had from the caretaker. The pretty village of Sedlescombe, it may be added, lies within three miles of Battle. How would our dear Brabby have rejoiced in the anticipation of such a remembrancer! It is to be hoped that its originator will find her efforts appreciated, and that the glorified tithe barn will especially attract scores and hundreds of the uninitiated in art, those who cannot run to town, just "to take a turn in the galleries," and whose art-education is in its elementary stage.

In his recently-published correspondence John Stuart Mill dwells almost solemnly on the necessity of cultivating the imaginative faculties of the masses. Writing in 1852 to a casual correspondent on the subject of teaching social science to the uneducated, he says—

"What the poor as well as the rich require is not to be indoctrinated, not to be taught other people's opinions, but to be induced and enabled to think for themselves. . . . They cannot read too much, especially geography, voyages, travels, romances, which must tend to awaken their imagination."

In France the idea, carried out by loving initiative at Sedlescombe, is being brought to fruition by village municipalities. Thus the village of

H. B. Brabazon (Brabby)

Bourron on the eastern border of Fontainebleau forest and described by me elsewhere,[1] has now its little museum, gifts by native artists and loans swiftly making up a very respectable picture gallery. "What," wrote one promoter of the scheme, "does not France owe to her villages— her greatest landscape painters, Rousseau, Corot, Daubigny, Millet and the rest? We all love our villages, but hitherto in this respect have quite neglected them. Let alike artists, *littérateurs* and residents combine, making of their modest town-halls artistic centres, thus developing in the peasant a love of the beautiful."

Our own local councils do not possess town-halls; the Brabazon Museum in the tithe barn should all the same prove an object-lesson. Accommodation would surely be forthcoming for such collections. Country folks would not grudge their threepences.

Mrs. Harvey Combe has set a fine example. The springs of charity need not be stayed; all the same our rich rural centres might surely possess their modest art gallery and museum. Flowers as well as bread might be dispensed by those overburdened with both.

[1] *East of Paris*, Hurst and Blackett.

X

OWEN MEREDITH—LORD LYTTON

X

OWEN MEREDITH—LORD LYTTON

An endearing personality and a charming host was the author of *Lucile*. It was during the Centennial Exhibition of 1889 that, with many other English visitors, I enjoyed the hospitality of the British Embassy in Paris. Official recognition of this great anniversary had been tabooed at home. "With the French Revolution and the Rights of Man," had cynically said Lord Salisbury, "the English nation had naught to do." As a private individual Lord Lytton, who loved France and was a very popular Ambassador, could appreciate the occasion. For myself, and doubtless for many others, his courtesy and friendly welcome then rendered a visit to Paris doubly attractive.

We were a numerous company at that animated luncheon in the Faubourg St. Honoré just twenty-two years ago. The gracious hostess and her beautiful daughter had received their guests, and we were all seated at table when the Ambassador, leisurely strolling in, took the vacant chair beside my own.

"Owen Meredith"—so I love to call him, and so perhaps he would have preferred to be brought to mind—was just fifty. Of fastidious rather than striking appearance, he suggested the poet rather than the diplomat. All the mental alertness of a gifted man in his prime was there, but not the physical vigour. Lethargic movements, an occasional look of weariness, betokened failing health.

Every one present was bound for the great show on the Champ de Mars, and at first conversation was general and topical. Soon, however, my host dropped the Exhibition, and we plunged into a literary *tête-à-tête*.

Naturally we discussed Ibsen and Tolstoi, just then foremost names in contemporary letters. I expressed my surprise at Ibsen's hold upon young men and women, his gloomy outlook upon life and suicidal pessimism being so antagonistic to all that we connect with youth.

"It is the novelty, the newness of the thing," Lord Lytton replied. "Therein you have the explanation. I can quite understand such enthusiasm."

Then we talked of Tolstoi, who, despite his beautiful gospels of universal brotherhood, has also penned novels as dreary as *Ghosts* and the rest. For *Anna Karenina* my host certainly expressed admiration, but measured in degree; his fastidious taste doubtless craved more of charm and beauty than Tolstoi gives us.

Then we reverted to fondly-remembered days at home, chatting of George Eliot and George Henry Lewes, and of their gatherings in Regent's Park, of Lord Houghton's extraordinarily cosmopolitan luncheons—"Dicky Milnes," Lord Lytton affectionately called him; he had ever an affectionate name for old friends—lastly of Paris.

"Paris possesses every variety of climate," he said; "you can get here the bracing, the intermediate, and the mild; you have only to change your quarters."

Here I could fully agree with him, at that very time finding a boreal atmosphere on the Boulevard Pereire, although we were only midway through September. In the neighbourhood of the

Tuileries Gardens at the same time the weather was deliciously warm and sunny.

Throughout my visit I could not help contrasting the objective with the subjective existence of the speaker.

Here was a man whose dearest ambition had been foiled by over-kindness of Fortune. Born apparently to a poet's lot, he became a diplomat instead, swiftly and with comparative ease attaining prize after prize. The gift by which he set most store was withheld: poetic supremacy he failed to win.

Yet his gifts were remarkable. Possessed of a charming fancy, a most musical ear, and a rich vocabulary, he has perhaps left nothing incorporated into our literature—nothing that has become part and parcel of English poetry. Nor during his lifetime did he attain the recognition of men far less gifted than himself. How came this about?

A glance at his biography solves the enigma. It is easy, as we read, to understand why *Clytemnestra*, written in early life, should have heralded fulfilment, and *Glenaveril*, published half a century later, should have knelled failure. Between the two periods in what a whirl had Lord Lytton lived! Entering the diplomatic service when a lad of eighteen, he became by turns Attaché at Washington, Florence, The Hague, St. Petersburg, Vienna, and Constantinople; later on, he became Acting Consul-General at Belgrade, Secretary of Legation at Copenhagen, at Athens, and Lisbon; later still, he filled the post of Secretary to the Embassies of Vienna and Paris; was named Ambassador at Lisbon; finally, Viceroy of India, and Ambassador in Paris, where he died. Under these circumstances, might not the poet have applied Matthew Arnold's lines to his own muse—

> "What shelter to grow ripe is ours,
> What leisure to grow wise"?

And throughout Lady Betty Balfour's deeply interesting biography of her father we realise a sense of disillusion; on his part a pathetic yearning and looking back. In the personality of the Viceroy of India and Ambassador in Paris, that of "Owen Meredith" had suffered eclipse. Born for the poet's career, he had followed another and wholly incongruous vocation.

After that first brief acquaintance in 1889, Lord Lytton and myself were in close correspondence. Struck with the charm of his lyrics and shorter poems, I prepared a little anthology,[1] in which he took the liveliest interest. Every note penned by the Ambassador showed in what a turmoil his days were spent.

"For weeks past," he wrote on March 28, 1890, "I have been wishing to write to you about the selection you have so graciously and flatteringly undertaken from my *disjecta membra* for the Canterbury edition. But my good intentions have all gone to enlarge that infernal causeway which is said to be paved with such things. A continuous stream of unexpected interruptions and occupations has been running between me and them, and the time has slipped by like water."

The letter, finished a few days later, thus wound up—

"These" (suggested poems for the little volume in question) "have been selected under

---

[1] Published in 1890 in the "Canterbury Poets" Series, edited by the late William Sharp.

incessant interruption and in desperate haste, which I regret. But needs must when the devil drives."

In April of the same year Lord Lytton acted as Minister in attendance on the Queen at Aix-les-Bains, and from thence wrote to me in a comparatively leisurely strain—

"Your letter finds me here, more fortunate than the American who complained when he went to a watering-place for change and rest that the waiters took all the change and his hotel bills all the rest. Indeed I am basking in a trance of idleness which is altogether delightful, notwithstanding the bitter cold of the weather, which has suddenly changed from summer to winter. Pray accept my cordially grateful thanks for your benevolent reception of that clumsy packet I sent you from Paris. The contents were the crude product of unavoidably raw haste."

Further on he spoke of the "woeful haste" in which he had dispatched some corrections for the anthology, adding: "The Queen, who is in excellent health and spirits, seems to be enjoying her stay at Aix—I dare say for the same reason that makes mine so welcome to me—the freedom and rest of it. For the weather, which was warm and bright, has turned dark and cold, and the place looks like a deserted village. Few of the shops are as yet opened, all the usual places of amusement closed, the very mountains shut in mud and snow, and with the exception of her Majesty's immediate family and official entourage, nobody here but Lady S. and Lady D.;" and he added—

"May I end this letter with a note of interrogation by asking you a question for which my excuse must be that I regard you as the most competent authority in Europe on the subject of it? Should you say from your personal knowledge of the French peasant that Zola's portrait of him and his—in *La Terre*—is a perfectly truthful one, free from all exaggeration?"

The selection appeared in October of the same year, and evidently gave Lord Lytton much pleasure. His satisfaction at seeing his poems in a popular reprint was, however, somewhat marred by the fact of certain printers' errors. Despite the store set by poetic fame, he had not found the necessary leisure for proof correction. But he heartily thanked his editress.

"There is a bond between us," he said—somewhat sadly, I thought—when bidding me farewell the last time I was the guest of the Embassy.

A few months later he died, pen in hand. He was engaged upon a poem when the fatal seizure came.

As an official of the French Government wrote to me, Lord Lytton's death was universally regretted in France. "Frenchmen," wrote this correspondent, "unfortunately divided about most matters, are unanimous in regretting your late Ambassador."

Every possible honour was shown to his remains as they were borne from the Protestant Church to the Gare St. Lazare.

I subjoin a few verses from one of the sweetest and most natural poems included in the little volume of my own editing. They are cited from "The Near and the Far"—

Friendly Faces

"Oh, near ones, dear ones! you in whose right hands
    Our own rests calm; whose faithful hearts all day
Wide open wait, till back from distant lands
    Thought, the tired traveller, wends his homeward
      way!
Helpmates and hearth-mates, gladdeners of gone years,
    Tender companions of our serious days,
Who colour with your kisses, smiles, and tears,
    Life's warm web woven over wonted ways.

" Young children, and old neighbours, and old friends,
    Old servants—you whose smiling circle small
Grows slowly smaller, till at last it ends
    Where in the grave is room enough for all.
Oh, shut the world out from the heart you cheer!
    Though small the circle of your smiles may be,
The world is distant and your smiles are near,
    This makes you more than all the world to me."

XI
HERBERT SPENCER IN SOCIETY

XI

HERBERT SPENCER IN SOCIETY

IT was in the spring of 1873 that I met the greatest thinker of the nineteenth century. What writer, no matter his field, has wielded such influence upon thought, what writer's works have been so universally translated? Not only in every European language, but in the principal Oriental tongues are his works to be read, the Synthetic Philosophy being now the possession of the entire thinking world.

My first impression was somewhat disconcerting. We happened to be fellow-guests at an evening party in Hyde Park Square, no literary conversazione, but something more than a gathering of cultivated people, among the crowd being several leading figures. Literature, art, science, law and politics were also represented by well-known, even eminent names. But Herbert Spencer was not to be found among kindred spirits. Here is the picture indelibly printed on my memory.

Standing in the middle of the room were two guests engaged in conversation, the one a fair, slender type of the Anglo-Saxon *ingénue*. She wore a simple, white muslin dress, as fashion then ordained, displaying pretty shoulders and arms. By her side stood a man whom at first sight one would have pronounced of quite commonplace appearance.

The founder of the Synthetic Philosophy was just fifty-three. Solidly built, of average proportions, whiskered after Mid-Victorian fashion, his figure could be called typically English. Only physiognomists would have at once characterised the head as that of a profound thinker. But, indeed, for the fact of recognition I might have passed him by as a very ordinary person, one of those numerous men of leisure who divide the day between clubs and society. Or I might have set him down as an elderly flirt for whom the *persiflage* with a pretty girl of eighteen was here the supreme attraction. But Herbert Spencer's life was of a piece, arranged on a rigidly consistent plan. Having lately carefully studied his works, and within recent years his wonderful autobiography, I could quite understand why in leisure moments he should prefer a very young lady's naïve utterances to serious talk with an equal. The philosopher's " Natural History," as he called the above-named autobiography, suggests the thought that, like Coriolanus, he had lived

> " As if a man were author of himself
> And knew no other kin."

In a purely intellectual or rather speculative sense, with him as with all great thinkers, it would naturally have been thus. A close study of the *Principles of Ethics* shows how the most trifling incident of social intercourse appealed to the psychologist. In a single sentence are often focused observations that must have been the fruit of years. Perhaps no philosophic work can compare with this great book as a manual of morals; and not of morals only, but of etiquette, which has indeed its foundation in morality.

From the *élite* of humanity and from human nature in its matured condition, the psychologist would naturally learn much less than from mind and character in evolution. Hence the magnetism of a girl just out of the school-room, and hence his well-known fondness for children. Here, moreover, is the explanation of an existence spent for the most part in boarding-houses.

I give one or two citations testifying to this Argus-eyed criticism of ordinary life: "To become a pleasure-yielding person is a social duty."

What sermons innumerable might be preached upon this subject! Daily do we see home life spoiled, firesides rendered uncongenial, family circles made depressing or indeed broken up by non-recognition of this duty. The very roots, indeed, of everyday comfort and happiness are here touched. It is not in everybody's power to be a good talker, nor can all of us boast of high spirits, sunny disposition or social accomplishments. But every one in the full possession of his faculties can curb a sullen or vindictive temper. The professional invalid, so often a blight upon domestic cheerfulness, is the product of self-indulgence. It is just by little ignoble defects and weaknesses within our own mastery that daily life may be not only soured but rendered almost insupportable.

But Spencer's criticism of men and women as social units goes much deeper. It is not only with right and wrong, with the altruist and the egoist that he deals, but with the seemly and the boorish, the delicate-minded and the coarse. Here are one or two quotations that show how minutely he had studied everyday life and manners, manners in his eyes ever being but another name for morality. In Part V. on " Negative Beneficence " we read—

"A game of skill is being played with one whose little boy is a spectator. The father's play is such as makes his antagonist tolerably certain of victory, should he put out his full strength. But if he is adequately swayed by the sentiment of negative beneficence, he will not obtrusively, but in a concealed way, play below his strength so as to let the father beat him. He will feel that such small pleasure as triumph might bring would be far more than counter-balanced by sympathy with the annoyance of the father at being defeated in presence of his son and by sympathy with the son on finding his father not so superior as he supposed. Though in this course some insincerity is implied, yet that evil is trifling in comparison with the evils otherwise entailed. In like manner none will doubt that he who, in a discussion or wit combat, might be easily overcome, may, even though at times unworthy of consideration, be rightly let off under particular circumstances. Say, for instance, that his *fiancée* is present. To show that he is ignorant or that he is illogical, or to utter a witticism at his expense, would be cruel. All but the unusually callous will see that to shame him before a witness with whom he stands in such a relation would be an improper exercise of intellectual power. An interlocutor who is swayed by due fellow-feeling, will, in such a case, consent to seem himself ill-informed and stupid rather than inflict the pain which would follow any other course."

The entire chapter on " Restraints in Displays of Ability," in which these passages occur, is worth poring over. To some purpose was so much of the philosopher's life spent in middle-class boarding-houses !

And in the second volume of his work under head of " Social Beneficence " occurs a significant passage. As we read the following lines we can understand how it came about that in an assembly of cultivated, even lettered, people, Herbert Spencer should devote himself to a shy, simply-dressed, simple *débutante*.

"Undue devotion to life and thought to the gaining of admiration by personal adornment, often brings loss of admiration. The feeling with which an over-dressed woman is regarded shows this in a pronounced way; and this feeling is excited, if less strongly, by many who are not condemned as over-dressed. For such elaborate toilette as shows the beholder that desire for approbation has been dominant, causes in him a reactive emotion; disapproval of the moral trait being set against the approval of the appearance achieved. Nobody thinks love of praise a fine characteristic."

"To be beautiful without manifest cost, elegant without manifest thought, is that which dress should achieve. Such an attention to appearance as implies a certain respect for those around, is proper; and yet not an attention which implies great anxiety about their opinions. A dash of æsthetic genius, possessed but by few, is requisite for success in this compromise."

It is a thousand pities that selected passages

from the *Principles of Ethics* should not be published in a handy form. No better treatise on the conduct of life could be put into the hands of young men and women. But although the writer's style is always crystal clear, like Rousseau he does not undertake to be understood by those who will not take the trouble to read attentively.

XII
GEORGE MACDONALD

XII

GEORGE MACDONALD

It must be thirty-six years since I spent an afternoon in the company of Mark Twain, and under unusual circumstances. The great humorist had joined George Macdonald's family circle at Hammersmith, not to amuse but to be amused, and the entertainment provided for us was the famous duologue of Mrs. Gamp and Betsey Prig, and other dramatic pieces, rendered by the novelist's young daughters. A decided talent for acting characterised these sisters, especially Lilia, the eldest. If I remember rightly, only Mr. and Mrs. Clemens and myself, besides members of the family, composed the audience, and in great good humour we took our seats. But how was it? The pieces had often been successfully acted upon other occasions, and before large numbers, yet, for some reason or other, matters did not now go well. Conscious of failure, the young actresses seemed on the point of breaking down.

Host and guest were equal to the situation. The host whispered in his wife's ear, and straightway a bottle of champagne was forthcoming, glasses chinked, healths were drunk, and a merry little *entr'acte* put us all at our ease. I do not remember a single word that dropped from the humourist's lips; what I have never forgotten was the unfailing tact and *bonhomie* with which the mortification of his hosts and their children was staved off, and a little social fiasco averted. Humour begets humour, and none present could afterwards have wished things to turn out differently. Alas! those three youthful actresses faded away one by one in the flower of their youth.

George Macdonald, whom I knew very intimately during his second residence at Hastings, was a man of many homes. Till his final settling in Italy, he had been a wanderer on the face of the earth; he, the most domestic of mankind, lived like a bird on the branch. Between the years of the acquaintanceship that speedily ripened into friendship, and his winter departure for the Riviera, his various homes can hardly be told on the fingers—Kensington, Hammersmith, Bournemouth, and Hastings are among the number.

When that good gift of £100 a year Civil List
pension came, which he enjoyed for the remainder
of his life, and a friend presented him with a
freehold villa at Bordighera, Scotchman although
he was, and Scotch novelist *par excellence*, he
bade adieu to a permanent residence in England,
and, let us hope, for the rest of his days
enjoyed freedom from daily, hourly carking
care.

I remember well one of his daughters telling
me with happy unconcern about 1872, when the
family, adopted children and guests, about twenty
in all, were packed into two small houses in
Halloway Place, Hastings : " Papa is writing two
novels at a time (each a three-volume one); he
gets through one volume a month, but he uses a
different pen for each." Just think of it ! Two
three-volume novels at a time—the mental stress,
to say nothing of the physical labour thereby
entailed.

Once about this time he said to me—surely the
most pathetic utterance that could emanate from
the mouth of talent or genius—" I have never
been able to do my best." How, indeed, could
it be otherwise? Eleven children to rear and

educate; adopted waifs and strays to do the same by, perpetual exercise of the most generous hospitality, and last, but not least, poor health.

By no means a strong writer, neither first-rate poet, novelist nor thinker, George Macdonald nevertheless enjoyed immense popularity. To tens of thousands, indeed, he was a second Emerson, a spiritual and moral guide, piloting them throughout daily problems and affording steady support.

It was in Nonconformist circles that his influence may be said to have marked an epoch, broadening the views of those who sat at his feet, lifting to higher levels alike their social and religious aspirations. One of these has lately written—" Thirty-five years ago I heard George Macdonald preach at a small Congregational Church in Camden Town. Since that time I have heard hundreds of preachers and listened to thousands of sermons, but the memory of that one lingers yet."[1]

Much of his teaching has long been superseded

---

[1] From a sympathetic and interesting lecture on George Macdonald given by W. Slade, Esq., at the Hastings League of Progressive Thought in June 1909.

by loftier and at the same time more practical ideals.

One of his addresses to working men, for instance, in spirit and substance amounted to a sermon I heard preached from a Sussex pulpit a decade later. The fat, prosperous rector was addressing a Labourers' Union, the first formed thereabouts at that period. "Remember," he said, "the beatitude of Scripture. If your portion is hard below, in your Father's house are many mansions," etc.

Whereupon the worthy parson went home to his dinner of roast meat, his port wine and easy-chair, imagining that he had sufficiently uplifted and comforted his humble hearers over their thinly-buttered bread and unsugared tea. Not that George Macdonald failed in apostolic brotherhood and love of humanity. Charitable of the charitable, he was ever burdening himself with waifs and strays, undertaking material responsibilities far beyond his means, in consequence overdrawing upon his mental capital till he became all but bankrupt.

But it was left for another, no poet, no romancer, no mystic, that one, to preach a beatitude of other kind. First uplift your fallen brother or sister, socially, morally, physically, transform the reprobate and the street-walker into decent men and women, before trying to turn them into saints.

"Don't ask your discharged prisoner to pray before you fill his belly," is a Salvationist maxim, a highly suggestive comment on the great General's career.

George Macdonald's teaching is not only nebulous, it savours of over-muchness and religiosity. Here as elsewhere he failed to draw the mean, to bear in mind Schiller's golden rule—"The secret of literature is to know what to leave out."

There are, nevertheless, things of his that will remain, maybe an early story or two, certainly some short poems. Who, having once heard, can forget the music and wisdom of the following lines—

> "Vex not thou thy violet
> Perfume to afford,
> Or no odour will thou get
> From its little hoard"?

Per contra, the much-admired little poem "Baby" is neither good poetry nor insight. Alas! would that a mere fraction of the final verse were true!

> "But how did you come to us, you dear?
> 'God thought about you, and so I am here.'"

Could a cynic have written anything less warranted by experience!

A sweet singer and a guileless, engaging personality, all who knew George Macdonald loved him, and all somehow understood the pathos of his life, of that unutterably sad yet resigned verdict on himself and his career—"I have never been able to do my best."

XIII
GENERAL BOOTH—A CHARACTER SKETCH

XIII

GENERAL BOOTH—A CHARACTER SKETCH

"HUMANITY lost its title-deeds and Montesquieu found then," was written of the author of the *Esprit des Lois*. I thought that the same might be said of General Booth on the 5th of July, 1904, and as I gazed on the tens upon tens of thousands of Salvationists making the grounds of the Crystal Palace black, all swayed by a word from their leader, I said, "General, there are two men you remind me of in your power of organisation and command of men—viz. Ignatius Loyola and Napoleon." The veteran leader did not deny the soft impeachment. Truly, after that pleasant tea in the club-rooms, the spectacle was one to move the coldest. Not a policeman could be seen amid those seething multitudes. Not a rough gesture, not an unseemly word met eye or ear. No sanctimoniousness characterised the great Army either, not a trace of the conventicle;

what struck the spectator was the robust, honest, good-humoured spirit of both men and women —truly a host of which England could be proud!

The absence of police and of any approach to roysterousness was, of course, attributable to the General's order. For one day not a single drop of beer, wine, or spirits was sold on the premises of the glass palace.

The final muster, the massing of bands and battalions, the cheers that rose up as the General in a motor-car was wheeled to the stand, were things not to be forgotten. Then the waves— rather, billows—of sound that rose up from the forty-nine bands! What pen can give any idea of these? General Booth has taken to heart Shakespeare's lines—

"The man that has no music in his soul," etc.

Men and women must have excitement, the matter is to give them elevating excitement; and how the musicians, gathered from the four quarters of the globe, enjoyed themselves—their audience also! Many of the Salvationists were country folks who, with their families, had come from great distances, having saved up for months past in order to take part in the great day's programme. And many had been social wrecks, degraded, brutalised, dragged by this agency from the lowest depths of degradation and despair.

A quiet tea in the club-rooms had come refreshingly between the monster concert of massed bands, forty-one in all, and the grand march past of the international battalions. And, being privileged with a seat at the General's special tea-table, I had a good opportunity of studying a most remarkable face.

I have characterised General Booth as a great personality; but, if I may so express myself, never have I beheld a personality so impersonal, individuality merged, lost in a single object, from any other point of view self being next to non-existent. I have seen and conversed with many men and women of mark during my life, but with none who so much impressed me with a sense of reserved strength, a held-back capital, so to say, of force and energy. At the first glance one was tempted to set down this weather-beaten, storm-tossed warrior as physically frailest of the frail; the silvery locks and beard framing a face of almost ashen pallor, the tall, attenuated figure lethargic in its movements. Quietly, too, unemotionally, he will chat for a while on his own subject. The listener is almost ready to conclude that this indomitable fighter has become quiescent, that his energies are fairly spent; but let some point of vital interest be touched upon, then his face lights up, his eyes kindle, his limbs lose their limpness, his voice becomes resonant, full of tone, " thoughts that breathe and words that burn " hold his audience spell-bound. The startlingly picturesque and original costume, too—braided coat and red jersey—well set off a figure Rembrandt would have delighted to immortalise on canvas.

In language every word of which tells, the General will recount some marvellous experience, or illustrate his methods by some homely but striking figure. And, whether it is the evangelist or the social reformer who comes to the fore, one is struck by his knowledge of human nature, his keen insight into the springs of human action.

Here is an instance. The subject of betting was touched upon.

"Now," said General Booth, "take a man who has only one shilling in the world. That shilling he bets upon a horse and loses. He gets another shilling, bets again, and again loses. But the excitement is worth more to him than the money. People must have excitement."

Music is a form of excitement that replaces betting in the Salvation Army; and there is no doubt that the part played by music in the work of social regeneration is enormous, for we must remember that General Booth's forces are by no means a merely preaching body. The plan is not to put new wine into old bottles. Salvation by the Army is two-fold, social as well as religious. The body is thought of as well as the soul.

"The point is this," said General Booth, after narrating some of his extraordinary experiences among the vagrant and criminal classes. "What we have to do in dealing with these poor creatures is to make them understand that we love them. Cruel, debauched, drunken, foul-mouthed, verminous : they must be brought to understand that we love them."

"Then you do not consider any class of human

beings utterly hopeless?" I asked. The answer was an emphatic "No," followed by a passionate appeal to all present on behalf of the self-abandoned and despairing.

And as I hearkened to that "old man eloquent," and watched his thin, worn features aglow with the enthusiasm of pity and his eyes fired with apostolic fervour, I began to comprehend his success—in one sense, a stupendous success.

Wherever the English tongue is spoken, in the farthermost corners of the globe, the Salvation barracks are now to be found, rallying-point of the Anglo-Saxon race, haven of rest to the exile and the wanderer, connecting link between the motherland and her scattered children. No other country has anything like it; no former civilisation can show its counterpart. By the side of this astounding organisation, all other schemes and systems having similar aims sink into comparative insignificance.

Yet not so many years ago one of the acutest intellects of our time devoted newspaper columns to satire on what he chose to call "corybantic Christianity." The Hanging Committee of the

Royal Academy permitted a caricature of Salvationists on their walls. A clergyman of the Church of England and popular novelist described the Salvation Army as "the phylloxera of Evangelicalism"; and, following the lead of those better instructed than themselves, bands of roughs at Eastbourne and other places beset General Booth's followers with clubs and stones, and even upon one occasion fired their buildings.

But the leader never for a single instant swerved from his purpose. Indifferent alike to mockery, insult, and molestation, he pursued his way, results a thousand-fold vindicating unshakable convictions and iron will.

General Booth has overcome all obstacles; at last his country-people fully endorse the words of the late King, who, in his interview with the veteran leader, congratulated him on the achievement of a work "of real value to the Empire."

And last year the indomitable old leader added his signature and, in fine bold characters, the postscript to the following typed letter—

"International Headquarters, London, E.C.
"15*th April*, 1910.

"Miss M. Betham-Edwards,
"Villa Julia,
"Hastings.

"Dear Madam,

"Many thanks for your kind remembrance and good wishes received on my birthday.

"The past year has been one of trouble, but with gratitude to my Heavenly Father, I find myself with a measure of vigour at the beginning of a new one, and full of hope that I shall be able to fill it up with work honouring to my Master, and profitable to my generation.

"Grateful for your continued interest in the work I am trying to do,

"Believe me,

"Yours sincerely,

"William Booth.

"How good of you to keep me in remembrance. May the best blessings of Heaven be with you. I have been *very* poorly, but am better, praise God."

XIV
VIDI TANTUM !—CHARLES DICKENS

XIV

VIDI TANTUM !—CHARLES DICKENS

"Ah! did you once see Shelley plain?
And did he stop and speak to you?
And did you speak to him again?
How strange it seems, and new!"

THESE well-known lines of Browning's will, ere many years, be addressed to all who, like myself, have seen him who is without doubt the greatest English novelist, and perhaps the greatest novelist the world has ever seen. What a peopled realm he has created for us—a peopled realm completely passed away, so entirely have externals, and, we may say, types, of the earliest Victorian epoch—(we must remember the late Queen's reign almost covered three generations) —disappeared!

[1] Of Dickens as a personality, a mere mortal,

[1] This paper was read before the Hastings and St. Leonards Dickens Fellowship by W. Crewdson, Esq., 14th December, 1909.

one of ourselves, familiar in his walks to most Londoners, my memory goes far, very far back. It was in the summer of 1851, when just fifteen, that I heard him read the story of little Em'ly from *David Copperfield*, at St. James's Hall. Fifteen is not a very impressionable age, and the marvels of London being visited by a country girl for the first time somewhat dwarfed this event by comparison, say, to Madame Tussaud's Waxworks, the sight of the young Queen opening Parliament, or the fireworks at Vauxhall. Moreover, the man whose name has long been a household word throughout the entire civilised world, was as yet only the most popular, the most beloved of English story-tellers. Here I will quote an apropos saying of a homely old aunt concerning a certain sister-in-law, who was weeping and wailing over the loss of a husband she had nagged at throughout wedded life—

"Ah, my dear," said this homely observer, "one must die to become a darling."

So it is with mighty spirits. Death and Time only accord a man his place among the immortals.

When with other young folks I sat through

Vidi Tantum !—Charles Dickens

Dickens's most moving selections, I do not remember being particularly stirred by the story itself. We do not easily weep over dramatic recitals at fifteen. The spell cast upon the hushed audience, the afflatus of genius, the communication of the reader's passion to his listeners, the overmastering power of a mighty spirit, who was yet a mere mortal with ourselves—these were the impressions which I carried away. And I have a very clear memory of Dickens as he appeared; the commanding but rather dandyish figure, then in his splendid prime, wearing black velvet, much-befrilled shirt-front, and sparkling diamond pin, studs and rings. Never did any man pay more attention to his personal appearance upon such occasions; and might not such dandyism be a kind of assertion, a protest against that wretched childhood to which he never recurred in speech, but which must have been ever present with him, and is immortalised in *David Copperfield?* Perhaps also the diamonds gave him pleasure, for Dickens was no æsthete. Human life stood to him for Art, did duty for Art, Literature, Science and the rest. But neither velvet coat, frilled shirt-front, nor sparkling jewels could detract from the force and commandingness of his presence. It was said of Burns that he possessed eyes of superlative brilliance and beauty. Never, folks said, had been seen such glorious eyes. With Dickens it must have been the same, his eyes matching Burns's. I well remember the piercing glance he bestowed upon some heavy-footed late-comers. And it is recorded that during his lecturing tour in America a look from him transfixed a huge audience, thereby saving hundreds of lives. The globe of a gas-burner had fallen with a crash on to the platform; the folks rose in a mass for a stampede, when Dickens, remaining motionless, mesmerised the crowd with a fixed stare; then, finding that he had awed every one, he quietly resumed his reading. The incident is recorded in Forster's delightful biography.

How different was the Dickens of 1851 to that of later portraits! In those early days of triumph upon triumph, of fame and wealth so rapidly acquired as to outdo the history of Walter Scott, he had not the lines, grey hair, and prematurely-aged look of later readings. I rejoice at having gazed on this giant of letters ere time had dealt hardly with him. If in dress, speech and attitude there might be just a touch—I will not say of pomposity—rather of, perhaps, over-weening self-consciousness—is it matter for wonder? In a world of snobbery, traditional obsequiousness, and conventional standards, he had raised himself to the very first rank, from that pinnacle of greatness surveying contemptuously, but not cynically after Thackeray's fashion, the littlenesses around him.

Dickens as a personality matched his books: he was great in every way—manliest of the manly as a figure, and of most imposing presence. Of the individual it might be said, as of Milton's Adam, "In himself was all his state." Not a scintilla did he owe to ancestry, patronage, or good fortune. He had developed without schools, stimulators, or academies—"As if a man were author of himself, and knew no other kin." Herein lies his singular, his unique pre-eminence. Men and women have risen from obscurity to greatness in various fields. It was left for Dickens to spring from the gutter, and not only to conquer the wide world with his pen, but to overcome malignant fate, leaving behind the memory of personal as well as of intellectual kingship.

I never beheld him again, for my early visits to London were few and far between; but how well do I remember the 10th of June, 1870! I was then living in a little street at the back of the High Street, Kensington, and had left home for the purpose of making some purchases. The first shop I entered was that of a stationer; on stating my wants, the shopman looked at me blankly, and without taking any notice whatever of my request, said in a broken and almost reproachful voice, as if shocked at my look of unconcern—

" Dickens is dead ! "

Never shall I forget that day. A great hush seemed to have fallen over the city. In the streets, shops, gardens, in public conveyances, people could talk of nothing else. As Mr. Justin Macarthy writes in his *History of our own Times:* " Men's minds were suddenly turned away from thought of political controversy, to a country house near the Gad's Hill of Shakespeare, where the most popular author of his day was lying dead. The news brought a pang as of personal sorrow into almost every home. Dickens was not of an age to die; he had scarcely passed his prime, not being far in his fifty-ninth year. No author of his own time came near him in popularity. To an immense number of men and women he stood for literature; to not a few his cheery teaching was sufficient as philosophy, and even as religion. Londoners were familiar with Dickens's personal appearance as well as his writings, and certain London streets did not seem quite the same when his striking face and energetic movements could be seen there no more. It is likely that he over-worked his exuberant vital energy and his superb resources of physical health and animal spirits. He was buried in Westminster Abbey; the national cemetery claimed him."

Writing to Charles Eliot Norton from Avignon in June 1870, J. S. Mill added—"The death of Dickens is indeed like a personal loss to those who only knew him by his writings."

It was really wonderful that Dickens's animal spirits and health of mind did not fail him, when we consider the terrible experiences of his early life, and after domestic disquietudes. His married life, if, to use his own words regarding Mr. and Mrs. Wilfer in *Our Mutual Friend*, it did not go to the tune of the "Dead March" in *Saul*, was not happy. Fireside incompatibilities doubtless account for the long catalogue of nagging "worser" halves in his novels—Mrs. Wilfer, the Ipswich magistrate's wife, and the rest.

I will now turn to quite another feature in Dickens lore—one not very generally realised. We hear a good deal about the Entente Cordiale now-a-days, and doubtless politics and writers of the last thirty years have helped towards such an understanding. Dickens I am almost tempted to call the foremost factor in Anglo-French friendliness. No English author, not Shakespeare himself, is half so dear to French readers. Translated again and again, his works are the joy not only of literary folks, but of the masses. A volume of favourite scenes was brought out not long ago. I know more than one French admirer who could pass a severe examination in his works. Here is a story bearing out this assertion. I had it from the lips of a French General of high position, who knows his Dickens, in excellent translations, as he knows his military code.

"When I was in garrison at Rouen many years ago" (this would be about thirty years back, he told me), "there was living in that city a dwarf who used to maltreat his wife; indeed, he used to get on a chair and beat her after the manner of Dickens's villain. This man was called Quilp, a few folks having read *The Old Curiosity Shop* and nicknamed him accordingly; the nickname getting current."

The same French reader considers *Bleak House* the best novel ever written; but for certain characters in other stories he entertains the highest admiration. Among these are Tom Pinch and Lizzie Hexham. On Dickens's habit, as was the fashion of the day, of introducing French villains, my distinguished friend is amiably satirical. No Frenchwoman, he says, would for a moment dream of acting like Lady Dedlock's maid Henriette, who punishes herself when in a temper by walking barefoot through fields of wet grass. His fair compatriot, he slyly adds, would be much more likely to deal any one handy a sharp box on the ears, or worse! Equally as a joke does this French admirer treat the French villain in another novel, *Little Dorrit*, which he says would be as perfect and complete a story without him.

Friendly Faces

In French garrison and public libraries, translations of Dickens are always found, twenty to one, I should say, to Thackeray's masterpiece. "The touchstone of genius," has written a French critic, "is geniality," and Dickens is above all things genial. One very popular French novelist, Alphonse Daudet, creator of the immortal braggart, Tartarin, acknowledged himself a disciple of Dickens; but his Dickens-reading country-people never for a moment admit that the disciple comes anything like up to his master.

In the person of the author of Pickwick it may be said that John Bull is not only familiar, but beloved by our good friends and near neighbours. "Never, even in Shakespeare's country," writes another French author, "has human life and individual character been delineated with more breadth, colour and feeling. The renown inaugurated by the *Pickwick Papers* has increased with time, not only in England, but in other countries. For ourselves Dickens's personages are familiar as our friends, his scenes seem part and parcel of our own lives."

It has been urged against his novels that they are overcharged with sentimentality; but, as

Vidi Tantum!—Charles Dickens

Dryden observes in his famous essay on Dramatic Poetry, "the genius of every age is different." As well quarrel with the coarseness of Fielding as with the sentimentality of Dickens! The one phase as well as the other were in the air when both writers lived. Of real pathos, without a touch of sentimentality, I will only note two or three instances. Search English fiction through, and you will not find three passages, a few lines only in each, that more nearly touch the deepest depths of human sympathy. I allude to the tears of Dick Swiveller when learning of the Marchioness's devotion; the meeting between Trooper George and his mother; and the scene in *Hard Times*, when Louisa tries morally to save her brother.

It is, of course, as every novelist knows, much easier to make readers cry than laugh. The cheapest pathos will do the former. I remember a very young man once saying to me : " What I prefer in novels are death-bed scenes." My young friend's taste can be gratified at very trifling labour to novelists. Death-bed scenes for uncritical readers can be had, like Gilbert and Sullivan's dukes, at three a penny. Real humour, true pathos, are the rarest of rare literary gifts; and here Dickens reigns supreme. Turveydrop making an elaborate toilet because he feels it his duty to show himself; or simple Pickwick, when consulted by his friend at the Ipswich election, telling him to shout with the crowd, "But if there are two crowds?" "Then shout with the biggest." The "If threepence is not respectable, what is?" of the itinerant showman; how delicious are such touches, hundreds, thousands of them scattered through his pages!

And throughout, alike in the humorous as well as in the pathetic scenes, ever runs a vein of humanity and Puritanism, the term used here by me in its highest sense. No tainted money passed those hands. No line could reproach him in his later years, except, perhaps, his ill-treatment of old maids and Methodists, so-called. Not for a single moment were fame and fortune sought by bemired ways. He lived in the open, and wrote alike for young and old, for wise and simple.

Dickens's gallery of feminine portraits has often been arraigned. An amateur critic once remarked to me sadly that there were no good women in Dickens's novels. "My dear sir," I observed, "you forget that good women in fiction are absolutely uninteresting." But the Marchioness was something better than what is conventionally meant by being good. Kinglake wittily observes of a celebrated and in his time almost deified statesman that "he was a good man of the worst description." Bread and butter morality, cut and dried virtue, are one thing; the heaven-born instinct of love and pity, making sweet and beautiful that which passes for the dregs, the heel-taps, of humanity—that is quite another matter. Dickens did not, for the most part, deal with the classes of society, who, if not good, ought to be ashamed of themselves; that is to say, folks who have been taught to speak the truth, keep their hands off their neighbours' goods and fair names, and go to church on Sundays. It is to his honour and eternal fame that he discerned the true man, the true woman, whose innate manliness and womanliness had, as in his own case, withstood degraded upbringing, surroundings and contact with human nature at its lowest. As General Booth said to me that the only way to get at the outcasts of humanity was to love them—no easy task, he admitted; Dickens also could feel sympathy, a touch of kinship, with those beyond the pale, and who are alike the curse and most often the victims of our social systems.

It is the fashion now-a-days to smile at the once much-bewept story of Dora, the child-wife. But Dora has only submitted to the fate of obsolete heroines, from Fielding's Sophia, who blushingly simpered out: "Indeed, Mr. Jones, I must leave *you* to name the day"—Jane Austen's Miss Bennetts, who felt life a burden when the officers quitted their town—Trollope's Lily Dale, who took to her bed when jilted by a cad—down to others of the same category. The type—we will hope so—has died out; but does that fact in the slightest degree affect the immortality of the portraits? Poor, silly little Dora lives, as lives Shakespeare's equally silly Helena, who hunted down Bertram and married him, wretched man, willy-nilly. "Nothing is great that is not true," wrote Lessing, the greatest German critic; and the delineation of Dora is great because it is *true*.

There is one class of English people—that, perhaps, the most solid, the most important, and certainly yielding to none in high moral tone and dignity, which this sovereign nature and mastermind wholly failed to understand. Dickens utterly misread Nonconformity. Inheritor, as he may be called, of Puritanism—so pure are his novels that they may be put into the hands of boys and girls—he yet rendered no homage to the Nonconformist conscience. The Stigginses and the Chadbands in his eyes represented what is now the pith, alike spiritual, moral and intellectual, of our nation. But again, to quote Dryden, "no man can resist the spirit of his age;" and he was a contemporary of Sydney Smith, whose scurrilous essay on Methodism ought to be confiscated. And did not that good woman and exalted lady who occupied the English throne for sixty years, and whose letters have been lately published, write in dismay, "A dissenter in Parliament!"?

One or two remarks only I will make on his works considered purely from the literary point of view. It is sometimes urged that Dickens had no style. But for what reason, in Heaven's name, did he want style? Did Scott, did Balzac, want style? As said Buffon, the great naturalist, a hundred and fifty years ago—

"Style is the man himself."

Could all the stylists English literature boasts

of, from Swift, Addison, Steele, Macaulay, de Quincy, down to the superfine Paters of our own day, have taught Dickens anything? The smaller literary fry have need of such masters; for the giants, the cross-row and the Bible amply suffice. For instance, could that appeal of Louisa to her guilty brother be improved by living writers of good prose? Could the ablest critic add, alter, or remove a word?

Differentiation in talk is one of the highest and rarest attainments in fiction. The late Samuel Brandram used to recite from memory many of Shakespeare's plays, never naming the various interlocutors. The speech of each proclaimed one and all. Now, if any one were to take up one of Dickens's masterpieces, say *Pickwick* or *Nicholas Nickleby*, and read a page of conversation, who would be in doubt as to the identity of the speakers? Jingle is always Jingle; Micawber is always Micawber; the inimitable Turveydrop is ever Turveydrop. We can no more confuse them than we could have confused Hamlet and Polonius, Brutus and Cassius at a Brandram recital. That novelist whose characters are not thus differentiated has failed in one, perhaps the first, essential of a story-teller.

Vidi Tantum !—Charles Dickens

One more criticism. Not for a moment accusing another great novelist of plagiarism, I can never read *Hard Times* without seeing therein the germs of *The Mill on the Floss* and *Silas Marner*, both works having been preceded by Dickens's little masterpiece. Unconsciously George Eliot must certainly have here found inspiration; and with all my admiration for her two works, I consider the history of Louisa and Tom more penetrating and more pathetic than that of Maggie and her brother; and Dickens's miner a much more natural and finer figure than the weaver of Raveloe. George Eliot could not help putting her own introspective habit of mind into her personages. Dickens put nothing in them that was not there. Hence his unassailable supremacy.

I will end these few and, on such a subject, most unworthy notes, by alluding to one of Browning's least-known but finest poems, *Sordello*. A man's life, he finely says, but in his own somewhat cryptic language, is ever—must be—finer than his life's work; the creator must naturally surpass the creation. From true works, he writes—

> ——" Escapes there still
> Some proof the singer's proper life was 'neath
> The life his song exhibits; this a sheath
> To that; a passion and a knowledge far
> Transcending these, majestic as they are,
> Smouldered; his lay was but an episode
> In the bard's life."

And nothing in its way can be finer than this man's career; his fearful childhood, his troubled domesticities being overmastered by manly cheeriness. Some of the letters to his son Henry, when a student at one of the universities, afford noble lessons to the young; whilst for his compeers he had ever an uplifting, supporting word. To a friend under cruel bereavement he wrote, after affectionate words of condolence: " We must fill up the ranks and march on "—march on as he had ever done himself, through days alike evil and good, in the paths of high endeavour, unswerving integrity, and fellowship with humanity, the least of whom was to him a brother or a sister.

I add, that to the Master of English fiction I owe early encouragement. In my girlhood he accepted for *All the Year Round* my narrative poem, " The Golden Bee," now included in Anthologies of our Council Schools and many others.

XV

UNE GRANDE DAME—
MME. (BLANC) TH. BENTZON

XV

UNE GRANDE DAME—MADAME (BLANC) TH. BENTZON

STRANGE yet true it is! Nowhere throughout the length and breadth of immense France do you feel farther from England, more completely shut out of Anglo-Saxon entourage, than at Meudon, a village within half-an-hour's journey from Paris by road, rail, or river.

I ought to speak of *the* Meudons, for there are three : Meudon proper, Meudon-Bellevue, and the poetically-named Meudon-Fleuri.

My own is the first, namely, Meudon proper, cure of the great Rabelais, who only secured himself against the Inquisition by buffoonery and licentiousness; scene of Saint Simon's immortal sketches, so many psychological portraits seized by the one pair of eyes Louis XIV could never meet unshrinkingly. So at least historians tell us. The Sun-king felt himself read through and through by Saint Simon's penetrating glance.

English and American trippers find their way to Meudon-Bellevue for the sake of the wonderful panorama obtained from its restaurant, but during several sojourns at the historic Meudon I never remember to have encountered a single tourist. Hither with her maid came the ever-busy contributor to the *Revue des Deux Mondes* during the long vacation. We lodged together in a ladies' school; except for ourselves and sometimes one or two other boarders, tenantless at this time of the year.

Madame Th. Bentzon would be busily writing till the mid-day collation; that over, and a little rest taken by us both, we spent the remainder of the day together, strolling abroad, calling on neighbours, taking tea in the garden, from which we beheld Paris spread before us as a map—and chatting always! It was not a perpetual duologue, for the *grande dame's* friends were legion, and one or two generally dropped in to tea. But for hours and hours I often enjoyed the privilege of a *tête-à-tête*, listening delightedly to reminiscence, criticism and anecdote, every phrase uttered in exquisite French and in a soft, melodic, untiring voice.

Une Grande Dame

Think of thus hearing one who had been George Sand's guests at Nohant, who had met Flaubert, who knew Napoleon III as few outsiders knew him, and, to come to recent times, who had visited Tolstoi in his Russian home!

But wholly apart from such glamour, and speaking not of fascinating talkers, how true are J. S. Mill's remarks on French speech generally! In his recently published and deeply interesting "Correspondence" he dilates on the charm—the habitual charm—of conversation in France, and which is not only characteristic of one class, but of all. Of all social accomplishments in France, speech bears the palm.

Madame Th. Bentzon—I ever addressed her by the familiar *nom de plume*—has been aptly characterised as *une grande dame*. This she was indeed, one of the last *grandes dames* of the nineteenth century. At the time of our Meudon rencontres she had passed her sixtieth year, and was already in failing health. Our acquaintance had ripened into friendship twenty-five years before, but if the handsome, vivacious, much-sought-after Parisian hostess of the Avenue Victor Hugo was hardly recalled by the holiday companion of the Pension Sainte Marie, added dignity, sweetness, and a most communicative sense of composure, more than atoned for vanished spirit and beauty.

Her life had been one of conflict and unintermittent literary effort. Married at fifteen, a mother twelve months later, and obliged to seek divorce soon after the birth of her child, proudly, conscientiously, and with quiet but highly honourable recognition she had lived by the pen.

Th. Bentzon must also be enrolled among the pioneers. With her great forerunner, Madame de Staël, she was a literary internationalist; and having attained the enviable position of contributor to the *Revue des Deux Mondes*, she introduced Ouida, Bret Harte, and other English and Transatlantic writers to the French public. For American literature and the American people she entertained enthusiastic admiration and liking. More than once she visited the United States and Canada, such sojourns supplying the material for volumes, if not profound or lastingly valuable, welcome and fructifying in their day. Her American friends were legion, and by the best beloved of these she was tended at the last.

Hardly less numerous were her *intimes*—alas! we have no exact equivalent—here, and about eight years ago she visited me at Hastings, naïvely including the little expedition in a paper called *En Londres et dans ses environs*, and published in her review.

Just as she had described the premier Cinque Port as being in the vicinity of London—a sort of Richmond or Sydenham!—so she was quite nebulous as to William the Conqueror's great battle.

Chatting at tea-time in my little parlour looking straight upon the slopes of the West Hill and crumbling Castle walls, she said naïvely—

"Ah, on yonder mountain,"—all my French visitors call the green hills opposite, *la montagne*—"I suppose, took place the Battle of Hastings?"

Madame Bentzon (*née* de Solmes) belonged to an aristocratic family, and had doubtless been educated at Sacré Cœur, in which establishment, as an old pupil once informed me, "French history ended with the *Ancien Régime;* after that —the Deluge." At what date national records began she did not say, probably with some such date as the arrival of Zacchæus the publican in the heart of Gascony! Afterwards canonised as Saint Rocamadour, his shrine is visited by thousands of pilgrims yearly in that most wonderful little town.

An event of such kind for the lady teachers of Sacré Cœur would naturally eclipse Duke William's raid with his sixty thousand filibusters half a century later; apropos of which a French wit once remarked to me—

"How your gentry can ever boast of coming in with the Conqueror is a perpetual puzzle to us over here, seeing that he was a brigand leading the scum of Europe!"

A devout Catholic, in political questions, like her friend M. Brunetière, a consistent reactionary, Madame Bentzon had ever the courage of her opinions. The following story, here set down word for word as related to me by herself, is highly characteristic both of the narrator and one of her great gods.

"After a long conversation with Tolstoi," she said, "he paused, and looking at me penetratingly, asked, ' Madame Bentzon, tell me, have you the courage to avow yourself a believing

Catholic?' I also paused. But I could not tell a lie. 'I am,' I answered.

"From that moment his look, voice, and whole attitude changed towards me. I felt that I had lost caste in his eyes, that he no longer regarded me as one to whom he could talk freely."

Constance, perhaps her best-known novel, shows the unswerving sacerdotalism of this warm-hearted, generous woman. For her, divergences of political and religious belief were so many fixed principles, she never allowed them to interfere with affectionate intercourse and even closest friendship. The heroine of the above-named story throws aside love, happiness, and is also prepared to fling morality to the winds, rather than wed an honourable man who, without lapse of his own, is divorced. Furthermore, she offers to live with him as his mistress, and thus become the mother of illegitimate children!—but for the scruples of her suitor and the counsels—mark the inconsistency!—of a Protestant pastor to whom she goes for advice, would have taken such a step. In the eyes of Constance Vidal—that is to say, of Madame Th. Bentzon—a Vatican rescript was the sole guide of conscience.

Friendly Faces

To a popular reprint of this story, issued fifteen years after its appearance in the *Revue des Deux Mondes*, M. Brunetière wrote a long preface, his introduction being not only a bit of French as perhaps only that great critic would write it, but at the same time as delightful a tribute as ever woman received from the other sex. "Formed in the school of *la bonne dame de Nohant*," he writes, "you have taken to heart George Sand's words to Gustave Flaubert: 'We must not write for twenty readers, for three thousand or for a hundred thousand. *We must write for every one who can read and who can profit by a good book.*' This, dear madame, is what you have done."

A great novelist Madame Th. Bentzon was not, and no author was ever more conscious of personal limitations or more judicial when passing verdict on self. Nor was any novelist ever more alert to admire those essentials of fiction she lacked herself, namely, *verve* and originality. It is as an interpreter of exotics, the critic and translator of Anglo-Saxon imaginative literature that she will ever be held in honour. As a pioneer in this field, the field of peace and internationalisation, her life-work has indeed been invaluable.

All the same, the long series of her novels may be read with pleasure and profit; neither realistic in the Zolaesque and Maupassant sense, neither ideal and poetic after the manner of her great forerunner and friend George Sand, one and all yet hold the reader's attention. Written in easy, elegant French, and always with command of a rich vocabulary, *Le Veuvage d'Aline*, *Le Mariage de Jacques*, and the rest, describe French life, not for *la jeune fille*, yet by no means for the reveller in intrigue and sensationalism. What they more especially needed was a distinctive stamp, the individual, indescribable, unforgettable hall-mark.

Of her own literary work, not from affected modesty or from undue self-depreciation, my friend never cared to talk. Praise, however, she appreciated, and on one striking little story—the last, I believe, to appear in her beloved review—she dwelt with evident pleasure. The *motif*, taken from real life, had suggested itself during her Russian visit, and it was just the sense of reality pervading every incident that held the reader's attention. Delightful *tête-à-tête*, oft-times prolonged for hours, and historic rambles—using the qualitative in an impersonal sense, every corner recalling the great past of Meudon—were not the only things to remember.

Madame Th. Bentzon, like all gifted people, carried her atmosphere with her, every day being marked by social intercourse, alike music and the arts being represented in these most genial and informal gatherings.

Especially on Sunday afternoons would the little lawn overlooking all Paris become animated. Friends would drop in from Paris, neighbours from the other Meudons, the alfresco five o'clock tea sometimes winding up with music and singing indoors. During the vacation a young American lady, an accomplished musician, had supplied a grand piano, her own performances and those of an equally accomplished vocalist—a young Belgian diplomat—making up a charming programme.

We had also for neighbours two sculptors: the world-famous Rodin, for whose studio my hostess possessed the open sesame, and the late eminent Gustave Crauk, whose noble statue of Coligny is one of the finest modern monuments that now adorn Paris. M. Crauk died a year after my last Meudon visit, that is to say, in 1906, and his appreciative townsfolk have splendidly housed a collection of their sculptor's works. The Musée Crauk does honour to Lille, no great manufacturing centre in France surpassing it in the richness and number of its local art collections.

M. Crauk's studio I saw in Paris, M. Rodin's also; the former, indeed, never worked at home, but besides his Meudon studio, his neighbour, that wholly modern and tremendously busy and creative artist—suitable impersonation of his own *Penseur*—has two Parisian studios, both sights to see and to remember.

But if a Titan in art, as a man M. Rodin is simplicity and naturalness personified—no formidably-overpowering airs about this great genius, no mystifying hauteur or aloofness.

Nothing could be more unaffected and cordial than his reception of my introducer, a lady and old American friend; but I must begin at the beginning. An appointment had been made several days beforehand, and knowing the sculptor's exactitude, to say nothing of courtliness, what was Miss S.'s surprise to find the two big studios empty, untenanted save by dozens, scores of works in marble and plaster. M. Rodin, the porter explained, had hurried out an hour before, leaving no message.

Feeling sure of his speedy return, we wandered at will among the somewhat eerie people crowding the two long, lofty studios; here admiring the bust of some lovely American, there the half-finished figure of the newly born, awakening Eve, on every side daring and highly original creations. What a contrast, moreover, to the traditional classicism of M. Crauk! Little wonder that the two neighbours failed to appreciate each other's work!

Then, in order to refresh our eyes, we strolled outside, M. Rodin having secured not only twin studios, but a bit of wild garden—turf, shepherd's purse, daisies and trees in mid-Paris. And whilst strolling up and down and admiring flowers, weeds and welcome umbrage—for the day was sultry—in walked M. Rodin.

"Excuse me, ladies," he said, after cordial handshakes, "but a sale of curios was just taking place, an object I had set my mind upon possessing was to be put up; hoping to be back in time for your visit, I rushed off to the sale-room."

"Not in vain, I trust?" asked Miss S., although her friend's jubilant air told its tale.

"Thank Heaven, no," was the reply; then *le Penseur*—so I must call him—and untiring bric-à-brac hunter took us round each studio in turn. It was a brief but fascinating half-hour he gave us, talking in friendly fashion about this work and that, patiently enduring our jejune encomiums.

"Amiability," wrote Herbert Spencer, "engenders amiability," and of this apothegm I had a verification a little later.

Railway officials in France always pre-suppose travellers' knowledge to be as complete as their own. Demanding a ticket for Meudon one afternoon in Paris, without troubling to tell me that the train just starting would only stop at Meudon-Fleuri, the clerk gave me a ticket for the latter place. Thus on alighting I found that instead of five minutes' walk, I had over a mile of unknown road to follow. The sun was tropical, and no shade was to be had.

At this juncture a youth—he was hardly more than a boy—came up, and hearing my inquiries, promptly offered his services.

"I am bound to Meudon," he said, "and shall be delighted to accompany madame."

Which he did, obligingly carrying my cloak and chatting all the while.

"I am M. Rodin's secretary," he proudly informed me before we quitted company. The youthful secretary had perhaps acquired that charming urbanity and helpfulness from his employer. An English lad might have felt the same willingness to help a stranded Frenchwoman, but would shyly hesitate.

Yet another year—1905—I re-visited Meudon, this time for a day only, a last, full and memorable day. For some time my friend had been in very parlous health, but she was still her old self, and still at work. Amongst other topics we discussed Gresset, whose monumental tablet I had just before inspected in Amiens cathedral. She brought out a delightful little edition of the unhappy humourist and made me read his inimitable *Lutrin Vivant*, then talked of the admirable and so modern play, *Le Méchant*.

At parting she put the two volumes in my hand, saying—

"Take these with you, and if you do not find me next year, keep them as a souvenir."

As we all know, Gresset was hounded down by the sacerdotalists on account of his immortal *Vert-Vert*, published in 1733, when a student at a Jesuit college. Quitting the habit later, he lived in the world, throwing off one brilliant piece after another, finally falling under the influence of an arch-obscurantist, a Bishop of Amiens; he publicly repudiated all his printed works, burnt those in manuscript, and died in the odour of sanctity.

Madame Th. Bentzon's little volumes, bound in leather with red edges, and having what look like royal book-plates without motto, were published by "Edouard Kelmarnech, Londres, 1765," at that time *Vert-Vert* being tabooed in France.

A few months after that September visit Th. Bentzon died, in 1906, having received the Legion of Honour, as she sadly said, "to adorn my coffin!" The tardigrade recognition, however, gave pleasure, and especially to her friends.

XVI

A GROUP OF FRENCH FRIENDS

1880–85

XVI

A GROUP OF FRENCH FRIENDS

FONDLY cherished little Gemeaux!—for so many years holiday home of its English chronicler, "an idlesse all the day amid bucolic scenes and dear but foreign friends, their foreignness lending romance and charm."

It is just upon a generation ago since that Chinese wall, the French dwelling here yielded to Britannic intrusion. Gemeaux to-day appears like a dream, so much having happened since those far-off experiences. The fifteen-year-old lad, who, during two wet days, fast as tongue could, read aloud novels for the amusement of his grandmother and her guest, is now a long-established advocate. "My Bernard is just preparing for his *baccalauréat*, and his brothers are fast growing up," he wrote to me the other day. The first and second cousins who danced together on Sunday evenings have all married and gone their separate ways; the ranks of their parents have been much thinned, whilst the earlier generation has entirely passed away. Doubtless the place itself, and, in some respects, the inhabitants, remain what it was in the opening years of the Third Republic. French villages, no more than French interiors, give way to love of change. Our neighbours, however intellectually fastidious, are not an expensive people—the worst machines indeed ever invented in the world for spending money, wrote the original and witty M. Demolius.

The fine old church, neglected alike without and within, the substantially-built houses of bourgeoisie and small vintager, so out of date as to convenience and accommodation, the furniture and fittings, deemed good enough for successive generations, the stock-still standards, mental, material and social, all illustrated a spirit of conservatism here and there in France proof against innovation.

In his work *L'Énergie Française*, M. Hanotaux somewhat paradoxically describes nineteenth-century Laon, the dead-alive little city with the superb cathedral familiar to many Swiss-bound travellers. The historian's picture of society here recalls Balzac's immortal scene. The fossilised

Guérande of *Béatrix* a century ago was not more stationary than is actual Laon, or my Burgundian village during M. Grévy's presidency.

For the first time within living memory had an English guest joined the little society; for the first time had a Protestant born and bred been heard of in the neighbourhood, a fact all the more noteworthy from what follows.

As at Guérande, as at Laon, here clocks hardly seemed to move. Time to these advocates, notaries and the rest was apparently of no account whatever. The long vacation, namely, the months of August and September, was an interim of almost superhuman inactivity.

Wherein, will some ask, consisted the fascination of this Castle of Indolence for an alert Anglo-Saxon, an untiring investigator of French life and manners? The fact is, every day, every hour was rich in impressions; the least little incident became an experience. Trivialities threw light upon national idiosyncrasy. Not the most cultured Parisian circles could so well have suited an inquirer's purpose.

Here are a few illustrations of my dictum— In Defoe's first-rate novel *Memoirs of a*

Cavalier, 1720–1, his hero writes from Picardy: "Civility is very much in use in France, and especially to strangers."

But the gist of civility with our neighbours lies in the fact that, as should charity do, it begins at home. Nothing more struck me during what I will call my French novitiate than this point. To Defoe's sentence above cited I should add—"and to seniority." The respect paid to age I noticed in all classes, even a rustic imp in sabots baring his head before his grandmother.

In Nadaud's famous ballad "Les Trois Hussars," one of the trio, on coming within sight of his native village for a holiday, learns that his love is dead. Renouncing furlough, he turns back, charging a messenger to excuse himself to his mother, *chapeau bas*, i.e. hat in hand. The touch is highly characteristic. Manuals of etiquette had appeared in France long before Antoine de Courtin's *Traité de Civilité*, 1671. Politeness, good manners, etiquette, have for centuries formed a very important branch of French education. In the collective circle at Gemeaux rules of precedence were as strictly observed as in diplomatic receptions. To our own free and easy, rough and ready selves the minutiæ observed among my friends would appear something more than superfluous. The members of the various families, all being related or closely connected, and all living within a few minutes' walk of each other, used to meet after dinner for cards, dancing and chat. Gloves were always worn by the ladies upon these occasions. Imagine middle-class English grandmothers and aunts putting on gloves before calling upon grandson or nephew next door! Artificial as at first sight might appear such ceremonial, I soon discovered that it had a vital meaning.

These modest country houses contained two or three families, in some cases each having separate rooms and service, the various members only meeting in the garden or after meals, in others, grandparents, an uncle or aunt making one of the group. Thus with one genial Darby and Joan and their growing up children were always settled for the long vacation both paternal and maternal grandmothers. The household, of which I may say I formed a member, was tripartite. Under the same roof, but keeping house apart, lived my hostess's son, daughter-in-law, and their boy.

Sharing the dowager's table and wing of the house was her widowed son-in-law, a man almost as old as herself. A third household consisted of parents and four children with only the addition of the husband's father. And when October came and the clan moved into their respective flats at Dijon, similar arrangements were maintained.

It will easily be imagined that only by aid of extreme politeness, reserve and self-control could such collective groups hold together. Among ourselves, a dual—to say nothing of a triple or quadruple—family circle would surely break up in a week!

Economy, ever a predominant factor in French life, and ingrained habits of restraint and courtesy render the daily sacrifices involved possible, nay, easy. Concessions to independence and privacy are more than compensated by saved expense, one roof-tree doing duty for several families.

II

Who would have supposed that this tranquil little seat of fairly-distributed wealth had witnessed direst tragedy, every inch of its soil having been watered with tears, not a homestead without its story of conflicts, spiritual and moral, and despair!

This epoch in Gemeaux's history is indeed its claim upon a chronicler, and it strikingly illustrates the thesis of a great Englishman written just upon half a century ago.

"The dictum that truth always triumphs over persecution," wrote John Stuart Mill (*Essay on Liberty*, 1864), "is one of those pleasant falsehoods which men repeat after one another till they pass into commonplaces, but which all experience refutes. History teems with instances of truth put down by persecution. If not suppressed for ever, it may be thrown back for centuries; the Reformation broke out at least twenty times before Luther, and was put down."

This Burgundian village, with most of its neighbours, to the very last man I found Catholic and Ultramontane. An intelligent farming woman living in the adjoining parish informed me—for whenever strolling out alone, I loved to chat with any one handy—that I was the very first Englishwoman and Protestant bred and born to whom she had ever spoken. And naïvely she put the query—

"Just tell me, Madame l'Anglaise, do you Protestants believe in God?"

In the circle I had joined, no Protestant alliance had ever occurred within recorded memory. The patriarchal group had kept itself as pure from heretical taint as does Anglo-American stock from negro blood. At Dijon, Protestants and Catholics never came into social contact. The theological line of demarcation formed a veritable equator.

I must add, that with regard to my hosts and their relations and connections, strictest politeness and reserve characterised their attitude towards the visitor. Never once was I unpleasantly reminded of my heterodoxy, not once did I hear an ill-timed remark on the subject. Were a question or two asked concerning the Reformed doctrine and ritual, it was ever from motives of curiosity or in order to obtain information. The peasant-born *curé* always welcomed a chat with me, and from the same point of view. To him I presented a study, doubtless as diverting and unfamiliar as Montesquieu's Persian, or Voltaire's Huron, to the Parisians of their period.

I now reach the illustration of Stuart Mill's text, and the gist of this paper.

Some fifteen years since, national archives, alike the rural and the urban, were officially thrown open for the purposes of research. Historians were not slow to seize such opportunities, with the result that floods of light have been shed upon administrative and domestic annals. Now-a-days, indeed, can French history be really written! Inert as seemed my Burgundian village from an intellectual point of view, it has found its historian. Before me lies the little work of a diligent and scrupulously judicial Gemeois, *Un Village Bourgingnon sous l'Ancien Régime*, par A. Huguenin, 1893, each statement of fact being gathered from the municipal archives. As we know, centuries before the Revolution, villagers deliberated on local affairs, voting the communal budget, electing the beadle and school-master, and discussing differences between seigneur and feudatory: hence the interest of such records.

Here is the passage which renders M. Huguenin's work priceless as a contribution to history. It is cited textually from the parchments of the *Mairie* or town-hall, in other words, the communal archives, the writer being a certain *Prieur*—a prior stood next in dignity to an abbot—named Guillaume—

"In the year 1685 the King, by his declaration in August, suppressed the edict of Nantes granted by his grandfather Henry the Fourth, for the exercise of the Reformed religion, so-called. This declaration being registered in the Dijon parliament on Friday, All Saints' Day of that year, I received at Gemeaux the abjuration of twenty-seven families professing the said religion, so-called, three hundred persons in all."

A list gives signatures to the number of fifty-four, the remainder being minors, the bedridden and the incapable. Now no less than three heads of those houses bore the patronymic of my hosts; the familiar Ultramontane circle, therefore, of 1880 had to the last member Huguenot blood in their veins. Protestantism at Gemeaux and throughout the neighbouring villages had been as completely stamped out as the reform of the Hussites and Albigeois centuries before.

Until that fatal action of a senile and priest-ridden despot and worn-out voluptuary, Protes-

tant communities had their churches, schools and
cemeteries in the Côte d'Or, living quietly and
inoffensively, as this Catholic biographer states,
and "affirming by word and deed their loyalty to
the throne."

The Revocation came as a thunderbolt, but the
outburst of universal indignation and despair
availed nothing. Immediate abjuration, or exile
and forfeiture of property, was the choice placed
before these peaceful vintagers and tradespéople.
Is it any wonder that only three families decided
upon the latter, betaking themselves to Switzer-
land? One and all of the Protestant churches
were summarily razed to the ground, and it was
not until fifteen or sixteen years ago that Dijon
possessed its *temple* or Protestant church. Until
that time service was held in a room of the ducal
palace.

Here it may be added that at that time—*i. e.* of
my visits, 1879, 1889—the French Republic sub-
sidised all religions held by its citizens. Thus,
whenever a Protestant church or Jewish syna-
gogue was built, the site was partly supplied by
the Government, partly by the municipality.
Protestant pastors, Jewish rabbis, as well as

Catholic priests, received State pay. In Algeria the Mahommedan population was similarly recognised. All this has now been changed.

In the local archives just cited are other items of interest. Besides the wages of school-master, beadle and bell-ringer, the commune was obliged to repair church, presbytery and school-house, also the village oven and fountains, the municipal budget amounting to five hundred'and odd francs.

With regard to church repairs a curious point is mentioned. The nave was kept in order by the commune, the chancel at the cost of clergy and seignory. Perhaps this fact explains the contrast presented by the two portions, the first showing excessive simplicity, the latter often super-abundant decoration.

Not without natural charm was this Burgundian village and its surroundings. Here is a picture of my old friend's garden; neither care nor plan in the acre or two facing south, a spontaneous creation it seemed, homely little self-made Eden!

Pell-mell, in direst yet most amicable confusion, vegetable elbowed vegetable, fruit-tree hustled fruit-tree, flower pushed against flower, each, nevertheless, getting plenty of sun and shower.

A Group of French Friends

The over-full condition of this garden was due to the fact that here one crop is never wholly gathered before its successor is ripe. When grapes begin to ripen, ruby-red gooseberries still hang on the stem; tomatoes are in full glory long ere the red and white currants are stripped; plums, greengages and peaches are in turn neglected for the small, common sun-ripened grape. The flowers seemed to bloom simply for their own pleasure, unplucked, untended, hardly glanced at —roses, carnations, zinnias and the rest took care of themselves from May till October.

But the vegetation of this supremely-favoured region requires a volume to itself, one district very much resembling another. Well may the French poet write of his native *terre généreuse* (the generous soil)!

XVII
A GREAT-NEPHEW OF DANTON

[*To face p.* 249

DANTON'S GREAT-NEPHEW

XVII

A GREAT-NEPHEW OF DANTON

THERE is no more engaging townling in Champagne than Arcis-sur-Aube, birthplace and home of the great *conventionnel* who, by a single vocable, thrice reiterated, saved France from becoming a second Poland.

The Aube, a river of especial silveriness (hence its derivation from *alba*, the white), flows under a handsome bridge before Danton's house, quays, tanneries, and barges lending an air of bustle and cosmopolitanism. Above substantial stone-built bourgeois dwellings, each with walled-in garden, rises a sombre, many-pinnacled, richly-sculptured church; beyond the suburbs lie vast panoramas, lines of serried woods, clustered villages, vineyards and meadow-land, the river making bright loops amid the green.

Piquant from beginning to end are my recollections of Danton's great-nephew, the late much-respected M. Hippolyte Sardin, *juge de paix*, *conseiller d'arrondissement*, mayor of his native town and *officier de l'instruction publique*. Our acquaintance began under exceptional circumstances. An English novel, the protagonist of which was Carlyle's "Titan of Revolution," had been dramatised by a French enthusiast living at Reims, the first performance taking place in the Grand Theatre of that city on February 28, 1898.

Naturally the novelist was present, and having learned that Danton's collateral descendant would be there also, Reims being within easy distance of Arcis, I had ensured an introduction. For this, however, there was no necessity.

Before the curtain rose, two figures seated themselves in the dress circle near my friends' box. Certain French callings are unmistakably physiognomic. Here beyond doubt was the expected *juge de paix*, with him being his *suppléant* or deputy. Introducing myself at the close of the first act, we immediately entered into lively conversation.

M. Hippolyte Sardin could not be said to have inherited a trace of his great-uncle's herculean proportions, leonine features, or voice of thunder.

A Great-Nephew of Danton

Of middle stature, regular features, and still adhering to the whiskers of a former generation, and of the legal status, he was typically bourgeois, fairly representing that class best described by the words "humdrum respectability." English writers on French middle-class life are apt to deny its quintessential characteristic, namely, a constant and ever-wakeful regard to conventionalities. Respectability is, indeed, the fetish of bourgeois France, by the term being understood domestic rectitude and a goodly provision laid by for children and children's children.

M. Sardin, although eminently representative of a humdrum section, was not himself commonplace. From ordinariness he was saved by a great tradition, and he lived up to the heritage, never for a moment forgetting that he belonged to history. At the same time, no Dantonism was affected either in speech or deportment, to him that tremendous personality remaining historic.

When, in 1871, I used to take tea with Goethe's daughter-in-law and grandson at Weimar, I heard the German Olympian always alluded to as " der vater" and "der gross-vater." Not so here.

251

"Danton," not "my great-uncle," was spoken of in our many conversations.

Meantime, there was a comic side to the eagerly-awaited play. Provincial Grand Theatres are not over rich in the matter of costumes and decoration. What was our surprise to behold the stage Danton in sky-blue military coat with tails, tricolour sash and top-boots—precisely habited, indeed, as a Bleu in the Vendean war! Nor were melo-dramatic incidents without drollery. By way of giving realistic effect, an aged peasant woman bearing seigneurial tithes in kind to the château was accompanied by a live donkey; no sorry, bare-ribbed beast, but the plumpest possible. Again, a fascinating lady of the *ancien régime* dashes across the stage in a coach and pair, of course to be set upon by highwaymen, Danton— the monster!—proving her rescuer.

Barring these trifling disenchantments, M. Sardin and, needless to say, the author greatly relished the performance. My companion's re-flections must have savoured of irony. As burst upon burst of applause greeted Danton's some-what flamboyant speeches, he doubtless recalled the time when the very name was a reprobation in men's mouths. And on that evening I believe for the first time Danton had figured on the Rémois or any stage.

All passed off well, and as some of the most blissful moments in human existence are due to transient illusions, I will only record that the author heard herself called for before the curtain fell. If the shout, "Author, author," is delightful in one's own country, what must it be when heard on the other side of the Channel?

The play, however, did not take the popular fancy in France; probably it was not sufficiently *pimenté;* it lacked the *nouveaux frissons* essential in contemporary drama. And in England more than another generation must elapse ere Danton appears as little short of a demagogue.

"You must pay us a visit in the summer," M. Sardin said next day. "We have a large garden in which you can sit and read, and you shall be left quite free and made to feel at home."

My second visit to the pretty little *chef-lieu* on the Aube did not, however, take place till three years later, when old ties compelled me to accept the hospitality of a former hostess. Fortunately, both for M. Sardin and his niece and

myself—he had been for some years a widower—
that it was so. On the very day of arrival I fell
seriously ill, and for nearly a week kept my bed,
being taken the best possible care of by my
friends and an excellent *médecin de campagne*,
no perpetual harper upon graveyard topics like
Balzac's terribly depressing hero, but a cheery
man of the world who seemed to prosper exceed-
ingly upon his absurdly modest fees.

The *juge de paix* lived opposite; fruit, game,
anything he could offer were at my disposal, and
as soon as I was well enough, his company. M.
Sardin would then drop in, relieving the tedium
of bedridden hours by the sovereign remedy for
almost all the ills that flesh is heir to, namely
conversation. The Revolution, Danton, Madame
Roland, Robespierre, could any topics be more
hypnotic to us two? For the last-named I
confess to a qualified admiration. Did not the
muse-loving *avocat* of Arras nobly plead for the
Jew and the slave, and did he not, as Lord Bacon
said every gentleman should do, love his dog?

Certainly those chambered days savoured of
piquancy. To hold receptions in bed like an
eighteenth-century *précieuse*, to be entertained

by a collateral descendant of the great revolutionary, criticism, reminiscence, anecdote, making the hours fly, here was a situation at least of considerable unusualness!

M. Sardin's seventy and odd years had not been entirely spent at Arcis. I cite an amusing story he told me of "old Dumas, the great, the humane," as Henley calls him.

"Whilst stationed as *juge de paix* at Compiègne," he said, "Alexander Dumas stayed some time there in a hotel." The bargain with mine host was this: the great romancer had bed and board—the best of both—free, and in return, like Turveydrop, he "showed himself," once a day. "No one was permitted to accost him as he took his airings in the park," added my friend, "he was simply to be looked at, his admirers flocking from far and near for the privilege. I frequently saw him discreetly gazed at by these pilgrims. The hotel-keeper doubtless was no loser, as strangers would naturally patronise his house."

The thought occurred to me how many humble followers in the great man's footsteps would delightedly accept an agreeable *villeggiatura* on the same terms. Just think of it! At least half-a-guinea per day saved, and by the mere gratification of harmless vanity!

But most of all we talked of Danton.

"Strange it is," said my visitor, "that the very best life as yet written of Danton should be the work of an Englishman!"

The speaker alluded to the late Mr. A. H. Beesly's *Biography*, a work now used as a text-book in our universities, and which may be considered a classic. Among tributes received from French writers was the high appreciation of M. Aulard, the first authority on the Revolution.

Danton entertained an immense admiration for English institutions and leaders of thought. There was, therefore, no incongruity in the fact that his best biographer should be an Englishman. "An alliance with England was the key-note of Danton's foreign policy in 1792," writes the historian just named, "a policy he had imbibed from Mirabeau."

Locke, Blackstone, Hume, Adam Smith, were favourite authors of the great *conventionnel*. Of high and varied culture, a devotee of Racine, Corneille, Tasso and Ariosto, our own literature perhaps proved the most formative influence.

What would not some of us give for one of those much-conned volumes? All have disappeared. "Of the remnant of giants," none have left fewer personalia.

Yet as soon as I could put on my bonnet and cross the street, our opposite neighbour had some precious and most historic memorials to show me. Then indeed I could handle objects not only of daily use in Danton's well-appointed household, but which had undoubtedly figured at many a memorable banquet. There were silver forks and spoons which, instead of heraldic symbols, showed over the owner's initials a finely-engraved cap of liberty and its tripartite legend—*Liberté, égalité, fraternité.*

What souvenirs were here evoked! I thought of the tremendous personalities for whom Danton's lovely young wife had set her table —Marat, Robespierre, Camille Desmoulins, Madame Roland, later, for the misfortune of France and the world, to become her host's bitterest enemy, the Girondists, veritable "noble army of martyrs," the brave but ill-starred Custine, and how many more builders and victims of the Revolution! There is a story that Danton's eldest

son—a child of four when his father's head fell—
quite well remembered one of these dinner-parties
at which Robespierre was present. The little boy,
dining, of course, with his parents according to
French fashion, had let fall his bread or some
other eatable. Robespierre, ever fastidious of
the fastidious, somewhat sharply bade him
pick it up.

Here, anyhow, was disproved that terrible
calumny penned, alas! by a really noble woman.

No "wretched advocate more burdened with
debts than briefs, whose wife declared that she
could not keep house without a weekly twenty-
five francs from her father," was the advocate of
Arcis; instead the busy employer of two clerks,
besides his professional earnings possessing land
and funded property to the value of several
thousand pounds. Danton's household effects
were confiscated after condemnation, but were
restored to his family by the decree of 14 Floréal
an III, and in the following year the value of his
entire estate, with forfeited interest, was handed
to the children's trustees.

"The service of plate," my host informed me,
"was restored intact with the rest, but unfortun-

ately little store seems to have been set by it as such; it was used every day, and bit by bit most of the precious pieces disappeared. These are all I have."

Then the heirlooms were replaced, and another even more treasured relic was brought out.

This was a beautifully-executed miniature of Danton, presented by himself to his friend Brune, that heroic general so brutally done to death by royalist bravoes in the White Terror.

By the general's descendants the portrait had been given to the family.

It must not be supposed from such carelessness with regard to the plate that Danton's sons repudiated their great father. Despite the opprobrium heaped upon the name they bore, they persistently defended it, and in 1846 conjointly published a memoir opening thus: " Nothing is dearer to us than the memory of our father. Our most ardent desire has ever been to see him vindicated."

Such vindication neither of them lived to see. François-Georges, the younger brother, died in 1848, Antoine lived ten years longer. Both men spent their quiet, honest lives at Arcis. Realising their modest patrimony, they here set up a stocking manufactory.

It was not till 1888 that Danton's statue, result of a national subscription, was unveiled with great pomp and ceremony at Arcis. Danton's herculean figure in bronze, with oratorical, "perpendicular" hand—to quote Walt Whitman—rises from a marble pediment; on the north and south sides of this are engraved those famous utterances that straightway became history: *De l'audace, encore de l'audace, toujours de l'audace, et la Patrie est sauvée*, and *Après la pain l'instruction est le premier besoin du peuple.*

And since my second and last visit in 1903, the municipality have placed a memorial tablet on the big, handsome house fronting the river. It is thus inscribed: *Le conventionnel Danton, né à Arcis-sur-Aube le 26 octobre, 1759, mort le 5 avril, 1794, habita cette maison du 13 avril, 1791, au 30 mars, 1794.*

Upon this occasion the house was let. I did not again find myself in that upper chamber, at the window of which the great figure was seen by his fellow-citizens night after night before his fatal journey to Paris. We are told how he would rise from his bed and, night-capped, stand there, doubtless cogitating those thoughts put into undying words.

"Does a man carry his country on the sole of his foot? I would rather be guillotined than a guillotiner," were his proud retorts when urged to cross the frontier.

Non eadem omnibus decora. Craven-hearted princes and courtiers might have set such an example. Not for men like Danton to hide himself from his foes.

The historic name is unrepresented, but a great-great-grandson of Danton was born at Santiago in 1901, and is said in feature greatly to resemble the *conventionnel.* Madame Menuel-Danton, daughter of Antoine, died at Troyes in 1897; her son, Georges Menuel, having failed in business, emigrated to Chili and married a Chilian lady named De Souza. Their boy is now an orphan, without fortune, and the last I heard of him was that he would pursue his studies in France, a scholarship at some Lycée being provided for him by the State.

Of the great revolutionaries, only the two

antagonists, Madame Roland and Danton, have left descendants. Of the beautiful but implacable Queen of the Gironde numerous great-great-grandchildren are living. The youthful South American who was registered as a French citizen at his birth can boast of an unassailable claim to such ancestry, his dodecasyllabic name—Louis-Antoine-Menuel-Dacunha-Souza! — may prove less of a handicap through life than the glorious six-lettered Danton.

XVIII
ANECDOTICAL

XVIII

ANECDOTICAL

SIR JOSEPH HOOKER

I ONCE spent a pleasant and most instructive afternoon with Sir Joseph, then Dr., Hooker at Kew.

But how well I remember the sleepless moments that the charming scientist and a friend gave me a little later!

In April 1871 we were fellow-passengers on board a small P. & O. steamer sailing from Southampton to Alexandria. Sir Joseph was bound for Morocco, his purpose being to collect the plants of that (at that time) comparatively unexplored country, also to get to the summit of the great Atlas, which he did. In those days the P. & O. boats were far from being the luxurious and mammoth hostels of the present time. Berths were arranged around the dining saloon, and immediately underneath my companions' and my own every night sat Sir Joseph Hooker and a fellow-savant. Long after the dinner-table was cleared—indeed, till the lights were put out—the learned pair animatedly, and doubtless most interestingly, discussed Darwinism. Under other circumstances to play the legitimate part of eaves-dropper would have been delightful and most instructive. But a sea life to the uninitiated induces somnolence, and to this day I remember those eager voices, the recurrence of scientific terms and names—must I confess it?—how, in my desperate attempts to shut out the sounds, I wished Darwinism and all concerned at the bottom of the sea!

M. BRUNETIÈRE AT HOME

An audience of the late learned editor of *La Revue des Deux Mondes* was a ceremonious affair, the sombre palatial building of itself inspiring timorous folk.

I confess that it was not without awe that a few years back I was passed on from porter to usher (or footman), from usher to clerk, from clerk to

under-secretary, from under-secretary to secretary, all moving on tiptoe on carpeted floors, and
was finally introduced to the editor of the greatest
review in the world. M. Brunetière sat at a large
table in what was really an immense library, the
walls being lined from ceiling to floor with
volumes of the review from its beginning to the
latest issue. Laying down his pen, he received
his visitor and gave a few precious minutes to a
friend's friend. Slight, with a peculiar, sensitive face, courteous to stateliness, speaking the
choicest French in the voice celebrated for its
power, the famous critic and unrivalled lecturer
left upon my mind a lasting impression.

And three or four years later that wonderful
organ was gone. With a wail of despair he
exclaimed to a close friend—"Would that I had
lost my sight, my hearing, any sense but my
voice!"

A history of the *Revue des Deux Mondes*
would make a deeply interesting volume. One
striking episode of its career is connected with
the terrible winter of 1870–71. Through those
tragic months, whilst Paris was completely cut off
from the outer world, whilst rich as well as poor

ate bread compared with which our prison loaf were a luxury, whilst all the wealth of the Rothschilds could not have purchased a cauliflower or a pat of fresh butter, regularly as before on the 1st and 15th of each month appeared the great *Revue*. No incident in the universal history of literature is surely more remarkable than this.

Of late years M. Brunetière had become an obscurantist, and under the guise of fiction a reactionary propaganda was carried on in his review, the legislation of the Government being severely attacked. This attitude seems, indeed, to have warped the great critic's judgment. Otherwise how account for that unhappy expression of his, "the bankruptcy of science"? The bankruptcy of science, forsooth, in the days of aërial telegraphy, the X-rays, radium, M. Pasteur's discovery of the silkworm parasite threatening the great silk industry of France, that achievement alone enriching the nation by two hundred millions sterling, the sum of Bismarck's indemnity, and how many more wondrous achievements!

Let us hope we may soon see changes in the

[*To face p.* 269

W. J. FOX

greatest French review. Until to-day, however, the same spirit is seen in every page, reactionary, anti-progressive, ultramontane doctrines being as ever in the ascendant.

W. J. FOX

As a writer in the *Westminster Gazette* (April 1910 [1]) observes, it is rather remarkable that the biography of a man who at one time filled so prominent a position should so long have remained unwritten. A great Unitarian preacher and leader, a trenchant pamphleteer and orator, an ardent social reformer, the whilom member for Oldham is hardly so much as a name to the present generation. The story of this self-made man and true friend of the class from which he sprang was well worth recording.

There are few, perhaps, who can conjure up the figure of that "old man eloquent."

It was in 1860 that I spent two days under his roof in Sussex Place, where, separated from his wife, he was living with his daughter, a clever

---

[1] Apropos of *The Life of W. J. Fox, 1781-1864,* by the late Dr. Garnett and E. Garnett : Lane, 1910.

artist, and her husband, Frederic Lee Bridell, who is represented in the National Gallery. On arriving I found a figure that forcibly recalled Gilray's caricature of Gibbon, so out of all proportion were his body and lower limbs. The fine head, with its long "silvery slips," the brilliant black eyes and benevolent expression soon effaced that first impression.

"You see, I am taking my walks abroad," he said, as he paced the drawing-room. I think that he seldom went out of doors at that time. Then, anxious to set the little unsophisticated country girl at ease, he talked amusingly.

"I have been debating in my mind as to a *nom de plume* for a series of political papers I am asked to write, and at last have hit upon one—The Detonating Oyster. What do you think of it?"

At dinner some dish was served said to be of doubtful digestibility.

"Never mind," he said to me, "if anything happens we will give you a Christian burial."

After a game or two of backgammon came animated story-telling. Bridell—alas! poor fellow, already in the early stages of consumption—very dramatically repeated a tale he had heard in Italy.

A man had murdered another and stolen his horse, the animal avenging his master by trampling the thief to death. This narrative his young listener afterwards turned into a ballad, "The Ride to Rome." Mrs. Bridell, a very talented, vivacious lady, next told a highly diverting ghost-story, how she had been almost scared out of her wits by one of her husband's white shirts standing upright in a darkened room. The feature, however, of that pleasant evening was Mr. Fox's extraordinary ebullience and vitality. The aspirant—I had applied for the post of his reader and amanuensis —was not found suitable for the post, and as she took leave next day, her host followed—surreptitiously, as it seemed—pressing a guinea in her hand. It was a touching act, for the household was far from rich.

Among the witticisms of her father, Mrs. Bridell—later, Mrs. George Fox—repeated to me these—

"The world is made up of men, women—and Martineaus." So highly he esteemed the intellectual gifts of that great Huguenot family.

"My own pedigree goes no farther back than to the reign of George II, my great-grandfather being his coachman—but he did not do his duty, and turn the King over!"

The little volume, "Hymns and Anthems," used in South Place Chapel, contains some beautiful poems by the preacher.

Here is a little psalm of life—

I

The Sage his cup of hemlock quaffed,
And calmly drained the fatal draught.
Such pledge did Grecian justice give
To one who taught them how to live.

II

The Christ, in piety assured,
The anguish of His Cross endured.
Such pangs did Jewish bigots try
On Him Who taught us how to die.

III

'Mid prison walls the Sage could trust
That men would grow more wise and just;
From Calvary's Mount the Christ could see
The dawn of immortality.

IV

Who knows to live and knows to die,
Their souls are safe, their triumph high.
Power may oppress and priestcraft ban,
Justice and faith are God in man!

LORD HOUGHTON

A kind friend, a poet of real feeling and spontaneity whose songs will live, a literary internationalist to whom esprit and sympathy did duty for kinship, Lord Houghton—Dickie Milnes as "Owen Meredith" affectionately called him—was also a wit, readiest of the ready in speech.

Thus a lady novelist, for one of whose works he entertained high admiration, had published during his absence abroad a novel slightly touching on Socialism. Meeting her at George Eliot's in the summer of 1871, he asked—

"Well—your last story, how did it go off?"

"Not at all well," was the reply, "the Commune and the incendiaries in Paris were against it."

"Ah!" was the quick retort, "I understand. Your book fell with the Tuileries!"

In the eyes of Lord Lytton "Dickie Milnes'" rank, position, partisanship, did not count. The tie that bound him to his fellow men and women was that of mind and character. At his celebrated luncheons, poets, novelists, politicians, were ever at their best, the host radiantly looking on and listening.

T   **273**

Staunch in his friendship, the present writer owes a debt of gratitude to Lord Houghton. Her modest tribute is paid to one who was among the first according the golden gift of recognition.

His famous witticism—"That branch of the Civil Service called the Church of England," should surely be followed by the words "so called," thousands of clergymen now holding preferments openly following Roman ritual and teaching Romish dogma.

DR. MARTINEAU

As lofty a moral lesson as I have ever listened to I heard from the great Huguenot theologian, then in his ninetieth year. The occasion was a commonplace one, a mere social gathering of Unitarian teachers and scholars, by whom recitations were given, with music at intervals. Dr. Martineau I had met some years, at least a decade, before, but how little was he changed! The commanding, thoroughly French face, the clear, sonorous, logical utterances, the piercing glance, were still there. And this is the upshot of his address to an audience intent upon catching every syllable. Whether some especial event called forth the outburst, I know not; probably such was the case.

"What can be thought of an advocate," he said solemnly, "who, all the while knowing beyond a doubt that his client is guilty of some abominable crime, stands up in a court of justice and declares his belief in that man's innocence? I hold such perversion of truth as a great sin, and thus should it be regarded."

There were neither counsels nor criminals in that friendly assemblage, many of whom were young people, but of Dr. Martineau it might be said, as Goethe said of his contemporary, "Under all circumstances, Schiller was great." Bread and butter morality, the hackneyed phraseology of ordinary pulpits, could never drop from Dr. Martineau's austere and eloquent lips.

TALKERS ALL, SIR EDWIN ARNOLD AND HIS SECOND
FATHER-IN-LAW, W. H. CHANNING

In that choice, but alas! uncleansable, pearl, *Tristram Shandy*, we read—"As no one who knows what he is about in good company would venture to talk all, so no author who understands the just boundaries of decorum and good breeding would presume to think all."

Well, I have, thank God, been much in good company and have yet here and there come upon well-bred folks who for the life of them could not help being "talkers all," and although I hold no disparaging theories as to "mere man," I must confess that the culprits have belonged to the other sex. I add that the greediest, most voracious, most speechful beings within my ken have been men.

I well remember a talking bout between a poet and a preacher, Sir Edwin Arnold and his father-in-law, W. H. Channing, which well illustrates my theorem.

Both men were personalities, and, leastways in their own day, centres of thought and activity.

As highly florid editor of the *Daily Telegraph*,

and later as author of *The Light of Asia*, the younger man had a very large following. The elder, cousin of the famous American preacher, was also, on a much more limited scale, a leader of men, his leadership being spiritual only. During my brief residence in London, 1867–71, I used to attend his Unitarian services held in an ancient red brick house, High Street, Kensington. There on Sunday mornings about fifty men and women met, their place of worship being an old-fashioned drawing-room, their only magnet the enthusiasm—I might almost say the inspiration—of the preacher. Little enough of those impassioned and improvised addresses could be retained even by an excellent memory. But a moving and salutary impression was always carried away. For Dr. Channing's theme would ever be of peace, universal brotherhood and of a Golden Age on earth, as he waxed warm his countenance wearing a look of transcendent faith and goodness.

The two men had occasionally met in London, and they now called on me at Hastings with benevolent intent. What author, young, old or middle-aged, does not hold with the Wisest that "praise is comely"? They had run down from town on purpose to discuss my latest book.

Alas! Not for five consecutive moments was one golden-mouthed speaker allowed to resolve his chords, in other words, to round his periods and complete the especial view of any question in hand. Fast as tongue could go flowed Sir Edwin Arnold's flowery sentences; equally fluent, but more sobered were Dr. Channing's interpolations, the expansiveness and a certain nebulosity of both speakers quite preventing their listener from following either. Perhaps, indeed, what both had to say would have passed through a sieve without leaving much residuum behind. But it was mortifying, all the same. An hour or more of enthusiastic criticism and hardly five words for the hearer to carry away!

XIX

THE EX-EMPRESS EUGÉNIE

1855–70

THE EX-EMPRESS EUGÉNIE, 1855–70

WHEN the Third Napoleon—so-called—visited
Windsor with his Spanish bride I was "improving
myself" in a seminary for young ladies at Peck-
ham Rye. The mistress wishing presumably to
inspire patriotic feelings among her boarders,
also amiably enough to give them a holiday, had
closed school-rooms on the day of the royal
and imperial sight-seeing at the Crystal Palace.
Where we stood or sat awaiting the cortège, how
long we waited and how far general expectations
concerning its splendour were realised, I have
clean forgotten. Of the intensely-anticipated
and almost countless excitements crowded into
a school-girl's long summer day, all but one are
as if they had never been, completely washed
from memory.

But that one!

Vivid as a coruscation blinding the eyes a few
minutes ago, present to my mental vision as if
witnessed the day on which I write, is the figure

of the Empress as she flashed by. For hardly more than a flash was the sight, half-a-dozen royal carriages jogging at regulation pace along the road before us. So near indeed were we that the blaze of her beauty seemed to leave a trail behind.

As we fancy we still behold a meteoric splendour only just seen a few seconds before, so that ineffable loveliness lingered when lost to view. Ineffable is the word suggesting that feminine paragon—the blonde Spaniard—features, complexion, eyes touched with the goldenness of golden hair. Under such a spell, who had eyes for the matronly little lady by her side or the pseudo-Napoleon, whose face was a perpetual mask, sitting opposite? The Emperor's white, metallic [1] hue was intensified by heavy, hanging moustache and dark, questioning eyes, eyes ever coasting round his interlocutors—to use a Shakespearean phrase attributed to R. L. Stevenson— as if endeavouring therein to read their verdict upon himself.

[1] A homely Scotchwoman who saw a good deal of Napoleon III when in 1866 he visited Algiers said to me, "His complexion for all the world, my dear, was like a pewter-pot!"

Fifteen years later I was strolling on the East Parade, Hastings, one September morning when I noticed a little knot of expectant folks, every head turned one way, towards the street leading from the railway station. Asking the explanation of a butcher's lad, he replied—

"The Empress of the French has just arrived from Ryde," and turned on his heel.

A few minutes more and two open flies drove up, in the first being seated a pale, middle-aged lady wearing black, an attendant similarly attired by her side; the second contained two or three travelling trunks and a few packages.

The pale middle-aged lady, with surface smile and artificial bow acknowledging the general greetings, was the shadow, hardly that, of the dazzling vision seen a decade and a half before.

Etiquette and the fitness of things doubtless aged, hardly less as far as appearances went, than cataclysmal circumstances and physical wear and tear. An uncrowned, dethroned, repudiated Empress, so-called Empress of the French, who had fled from her palace by the help of an American dentist, must forsooth wear the plainest possible gown, discard liveried servants and use a hackney carriage. *Noblesse oblige* is a motto never lost sight of by monarchs involuntarily retired from business. One and all—perhaps the most effective teaching of their careers —they meet misfortune bravely. To show "shame of face" has been out of date since Sennacherib's downfall.

The Empress was soon after her arrival joined by the little prince and his tutor, and for many weeks the trio stayed in a cheap, quiet little hotel near the Fishmarket, in what indeed has been described as the Wapping end of Hastings. In fine weather the little party would climb the East Hill, evidently enjoying the fine air and splendid view. No one intruded on their privacy, their presence was considerately—or it might be from indifference—ignored, and on the eve of departure the unfortunate heir of the Bonapartes visited the mayor, thanking him for the privacy thus enjoyed.

The little hotel no longer exists, and on the sale of effects a pair of miniature busts, Emperor and Empress in bronze, was purchased for a few shillings, whilom gift of the latter to her host before departure.

XX
A TRIO OF PIONEERS

XX

A TRIO OF PIONEERS

THREE noble pioneers, each in a quite different field, each of whom at one time I saw much, here deserve many pages. But the careers alike of Rose Davenport-Hill, Frances Power Cobbe, and Elizabeth Blackwell, M.D., have been already told and re-told by more competent hands. I will therefore only say of these good friends a very few words.

Were any of my sex—except foreign opera singers—decreed a niche in the national Walhalla, the above-named trio should surely be there commemorated, Catherine Booth, the apostolic mother of the Salvation Army, and Josephine Butler, friend of the fallen, keeping them company.

We must not hope for such recognition at the hands of Dean and Chapter. Well might a Frenchwoman to whom I was introducing the Poets' Corner in 1896 exclaim with amazement—

"George Eliot, Charlotte Brontë, Elizabeth Barrett Browning absent—the only woman of the

Victorian epoch memorialised within these walls a foreign opera singer!"

A benevolent, admirable woman in her way was "the Swedish Nightingale," and her voice was a goodly gift of nature. What tittle of a claim, in Heaven's name, had Jenny Lind, afterwards Frau Goldschmidt, to Westminster Abbey?

The greatest thinker of the nineteenth century, one of its most illustrious novelists—a poet famous as those two, shut out of the national Pantheon! an alien *prima donna* being adjudged worthier of place therein by sacerdotal authorities! What will posterity think of the anomaly?

My almost life-long friend, Rose Davenport-Hill, belonged to that innumerable clan of Hills headed by their chieftain the great Sir Rowland. Without tale are the public workers of this veritable tribe, and without tale—*i. e.* innumerable—are the family ramifications. There are Davenport-Hills, Birkbeck-Hills, Berkeley-Hills, also Australian Hills, these again subdivided by affixes.

And one of the second dynasty, herself an indefatigable pioneer, is still among us, let us hope to live yet many beneficent, happy, and beloved years.   Florence Davenport-Hill (daughter of the well-known eminent Recorder of Birmingham) will ever be remembered as the friend and champion of workhouse children, and later on as an active supporter of Children's Courts.   She also for many years filled the office of guardian of the poor.

My business here, however, is not with contemporaries.

Her sister's work on the London School Board is too well known to educationalists to need recapitulation.   One of several women elected to the first body, greatly to J. S. Mill's rejoicing (see his recently published " Correspondence," 2 vols., 1911), she retained her seat for many years, aiding the cause of national education with unfailing devotion, ploddingness and, marvellous to relate, gusto !

Therein lay the gist of her career.   To this enthusiast came no disillusion.   The School Board remained dear and engaging to the last. Day after day she would set out from Belsize Avenue, neither hail, rain, snow or blow, nor blackness Tartarean damping her ardour, returning to the seven o'clock dinner as alert as when starting, and ever with something piquant to relate. The humour of routine and red tape would be delight-fully brought out by one who nevertheless was herself a routinist. No innovator, no inventor, was this loyal member; her business, as she used to say, was to support the policy of the Board. This was ever done whole-heartedly and from high standpoints.

Her wit would occasionally enliven very sleepy sittings. As she never made unnecessary speeches, she used to put a piece of knitting in her bag, plying her needles whilst listening. On being criticised for such unconventional proceeding, Miss Davenport-Hill remarked—

" This is the first time that I remember hearing of a woman reproached for using her tongue too little and her hands too much."

As a constant visitor to the Brentford Industrial Schools, her work was more especially valuable. And with what a glow she must have received the many tributes from "old boys" in after years! Not many months before her death one of these wrote from the Colonies—"You have been as a mother to me, and my start in life and present well-being are your doing." Could any fame or applause bring greater satisfaction to a public worker, especially to a Hill!

Of Elizabeth Blackwell, for the past thirty years my Hastings neighbour and anteriorly my good friend, there is little new to say. Her early struggles as a medical student are well known to all interested in the subject of woman doctors, and have been modestly but tellingly told by herself in a volume well meriting reprint (*Pioneer Work :* Longmans).

As has repeatedly been the case with her friend Barbara Leigh Smith Bodichon, the laurels of her winning have been placed on other brows. And now, " being very patient being dead," unless her biographical record is very carefully prepared, the same mistakes are sure to recur.

One incident of this most honourable career, perhaps new to many, I will mention.

When three-quarters of a century ago a handsome Civil List Pension—I believe of £300 a year —was offered to Harriet Martineau, she made the dignified reply that, whilst most grateful to Her Majesty's Government, the labours of earlier years had enabled her to provide for her old age. Elizabeth Blackwell, who began life as a teacher of the pianoforte, thereby supporting her younger sisters, could have made an identical reply to similar overtures. Retiring from practice soon after reaching her sixtieth year, she purchased a pretty little residence at Hastings, therein enjoying ease and dignity for yet another generation. No woman of Victoria's reign has bequeathed a finer, more practical, more disinterested lesson to her younger sisters.

The wise and witty "Bagshot" of the *Westminster Gazette* lately disserted with much finesse and pertinence on "the happy ending."

Frances Power Cobbe's life-story is an illustration of the felicitous *dénouement*, the happy ending. Most of us know how she devoted herself to the cause of helpless animals—in other words, the cause of anti-vivisection. With indomitable courage and unshaken faith she pursued her way, having taken to heart the Platonic, the final lesson—"As you properly conceive light and sight to be like the sun but not to be the sun, so you must conceive knowledge and truth to be of the nature of the Supreme Good, but not either the one or other of them to be that Supreme

Good" (*Republic*, Book VI, Whewell's Translation). I have ever held this passage of Plato an unanswerable argument against vivisection in any form.

Impaired health, loss of a beloved life-long companion, diminished income, could not depress such a nature as hers, but "the happy ending" came welcomely all the same.

One morning she opened a letter from an unknown solicitor saying that a deceased client, like herself, an ardent anti-vivisectionist, had bequeathed her a handsome fortune. So for the rest of her days, not only could she enjoy ease, comfort, and the luxury of benevolence, but also the power of propaganda. The capital at her death was willed to the cause for which she had sacrificed so much.

Not very long before the end came I received an affectionate mid-winter invitation to her Welsh retreat, one of the many invitations, alas! most regretfully refused by me of late years. North Wales in the season of snowfalls! Not even the blazing logs and geniality of such a hostess could have warmed me there in December.

But how happy we should have been together!

With what quips, cranks and wanton wiles should I have been beguiled! What interminable talks of old friends, old travel, and of the causes so dear to both! And we appreciated each other—that being once said of intercourse, all is said!

I cannot do better than precede my colophon with this noble life-story of "the happy ending."

THE END